FRANCE
BELGIUM & THE NETHERLANDS

Contents

Map pages	II
Map symbols	III
Route planner	IV
Distance chart	1
Road atlas	2-44
Index and city environs plans	45-60

Amsterdam	45	Luxembourg	52
Brussel/Bruxelles	47	Paris	54-55

4th edition May 2004

© Automobile Association Developments Limited 2004

Original edition printed 1996

 This product includes mapping data licensed from Ordnance Survey® with the permission of the Controller of Her Majesty's Stationery Office. © Crown copyright 2004. All rights reserved. Licence number 399221.

Published by AA Publishing (a trading name of Automobile Association Developments Limited, whose registered office is Millstream, Maidenhead Road, Windsor, Berkshire SL4 5GD, UK. Registered number 1878835).

Mapping produced by the Cartography Department of The Automobile Association. This atlas has been compiled and produced from the Automaps database utilising electronic and computer technology (A02029).

ISBN 0 7495 4120 2

A CIP catalogue for this book is available from The British Library.

Printed in Britain by Scotprint, Haddington, Scotland.

The contents of this atlas are believed to be correct at the time of the latest revision. However, the publishers cannot be held responsible for loss occasioned to any person acting or refraining from action as a result of any material in this atlas, nor for any errors, omissions or changes in such material. This does not affect your statutory rights. The publishers would welcome information to correct any errors or omissions and to keep this atlas up to date. Please write to the Cartographic Editor, Publishing Division, The Automobile Association, Fanum House, Basing View, Basingstoke, Hampshire RG21 4EA, UK.

Map pages

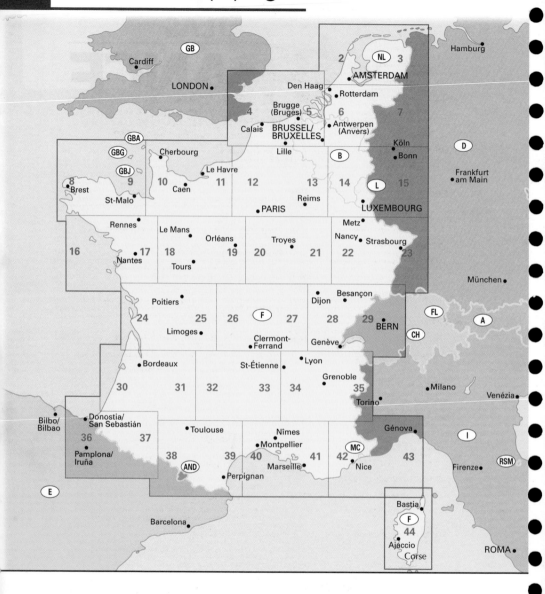

A Austria	**F** France	**GBA** Alderney	**MC** Monaco
AND Andorra	**FL** Liechtenstein	**GBG** Guernsey	**NL** The Netherlands
B Belgium	**GB** United Kingdom of Great Britain and Northern Ireland	**GBJ** Jersey	**RSM** San Marino
CH Switzerland		**I** Italy	
D Germany		**L** Luxembourg	
E Spain			

Map symbols

III

Toll motorways

A6 / E15	Dual carriageway with road numbers
	Single carriageway
●—12	Interchange
●—12	Restricted interchange
Ⓢ	Service area
══════	Under construction

Non-toll motorways

A15 / E31	Dual carriageway with road numbers
	Single carriageway
●—12	Interchange
●—12	Restricted interchange
Ⓢ	Service area
══════	Under construction

National roads

N10	Dual carriageway with road number
	Single carriageway

Regional roads

N10	Dual carriageway with road number
	Single carriageway

Local roads

N42	Dual carriageway with road number
	Single carriageway
D2	Minor road with road number

26	Page overlap and number

Symbols

E15 E50	European international network numbers
≡═══≡	Motorway in tunnel
─╫═══╪─	Road in tunnel
══════	Road under construction
	Toll point
▼ 63 ▼ 23 ▼	Distances in kilometres
══»»──	Gradient 14% and over
══»──	Gradient 6%-13%
Col de la Croix de Fer ─»─◄─ 2067 11-5	Mountain pass with closure period
	Panoramic routes
Bastia	Ferry route with car transportation (all year)
─┤───├─	Railway and tunnel
	National park, natural reserve
⊕	International Airport
⋔ ⋈	Religious building; Castle
⚑ ∴	Monument; Ruins, archaeological area
☀ ☀	Viewpoint (180° or 360°)
Ω	Cave
✳	Natural curiosity
★	Other curiosity
PARIS	Town or place of great tourist interest
Carnac	Interesting town or place
St-Lô	Other tourist town or place

Boundaries

━━━─·─·	International
▬▬▬▬▬	Internal

Scale

1 : 1 000 000

10 kilometres : 1 centimetre

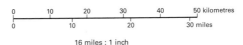

16 miles : 1 inch

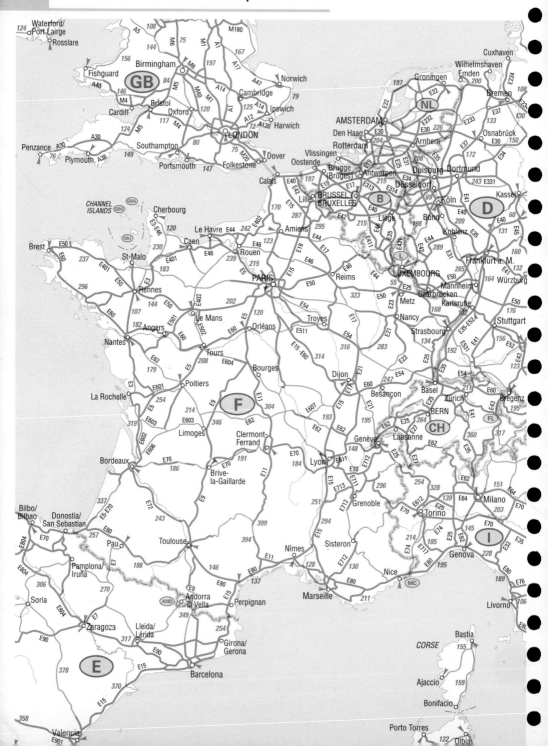

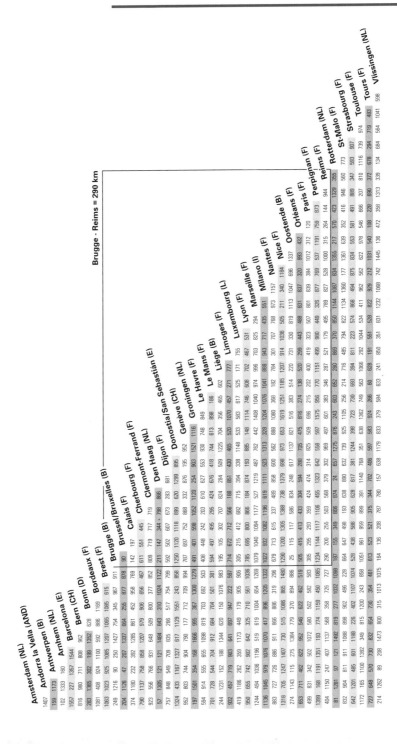

Brugge - Reims = 290 km

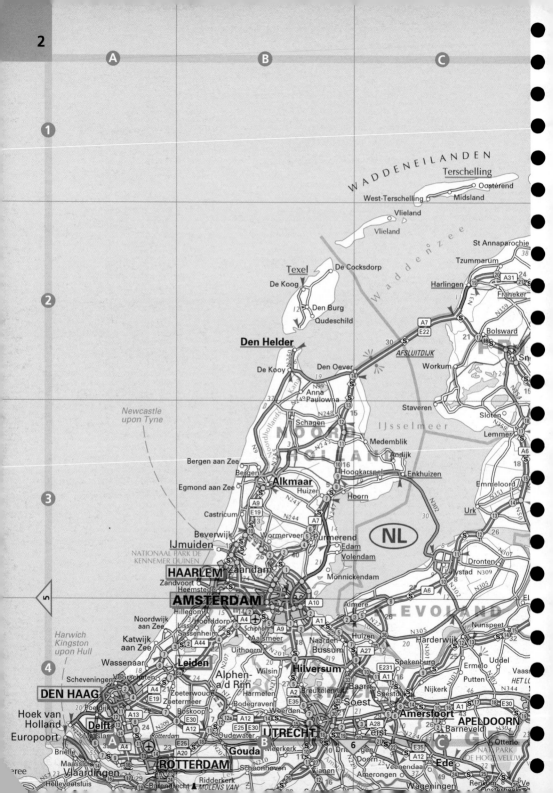

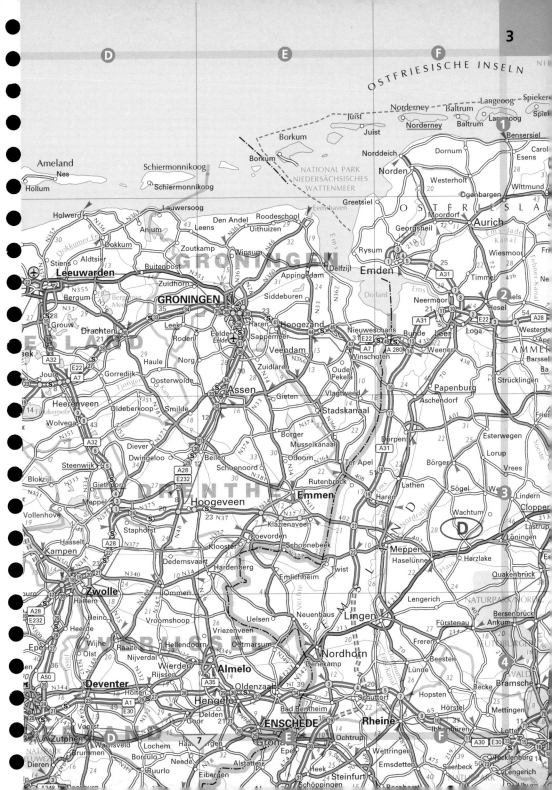

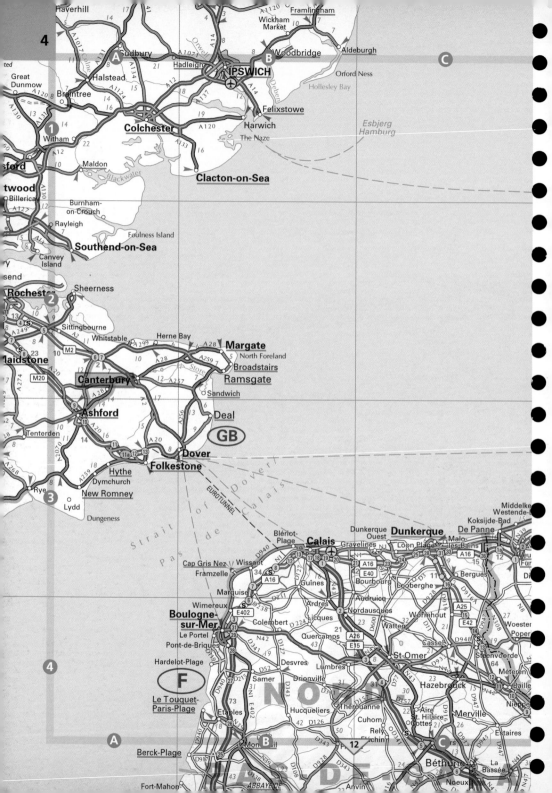

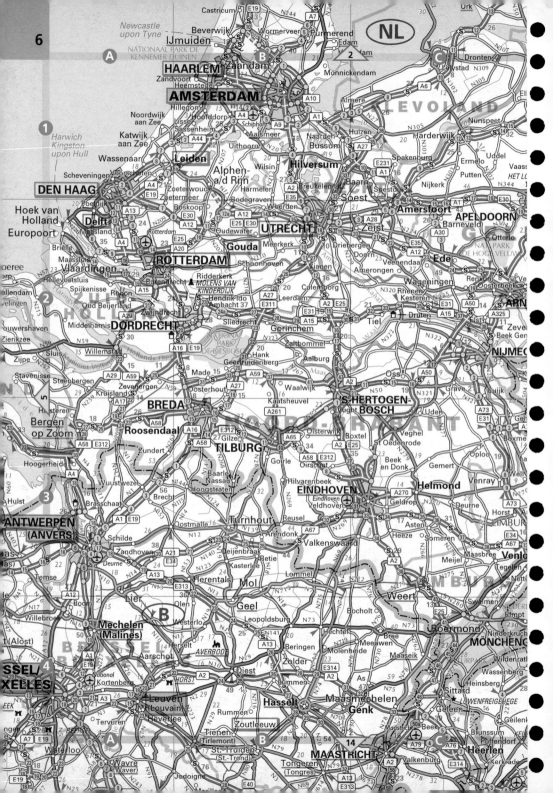

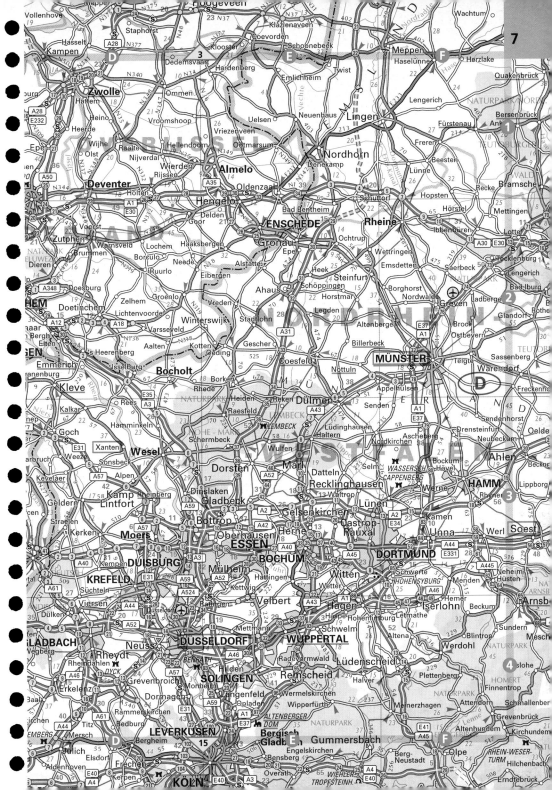

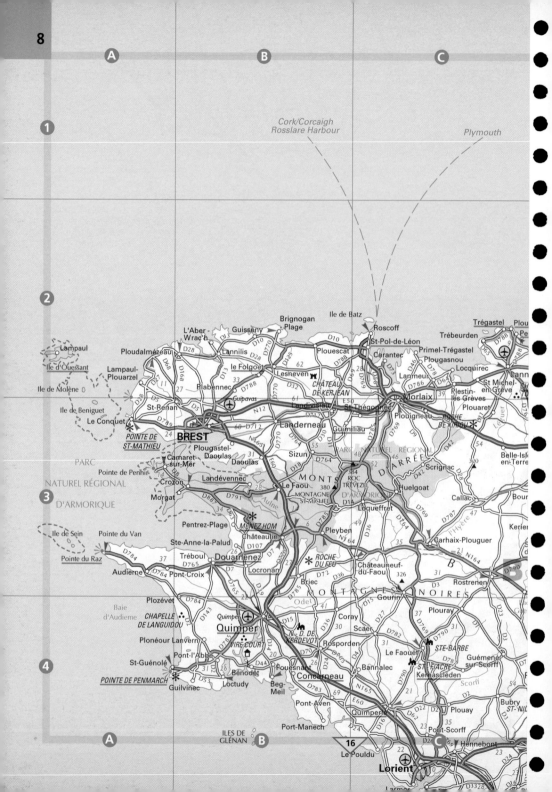

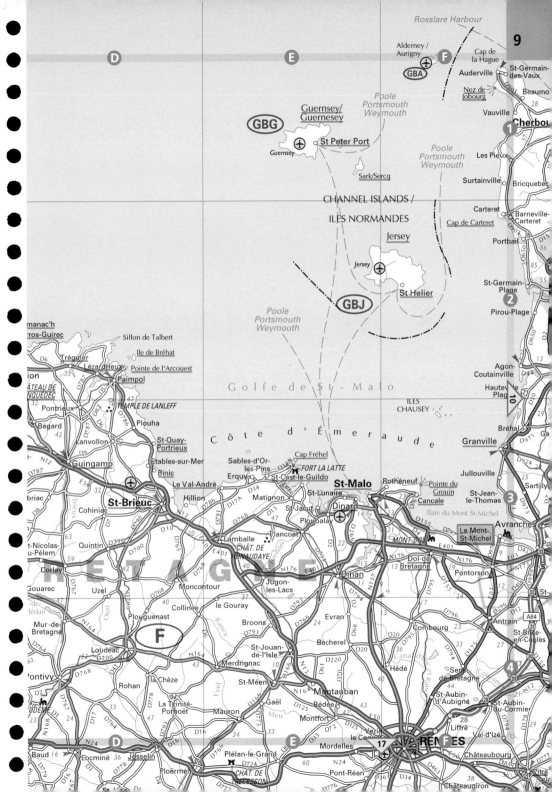

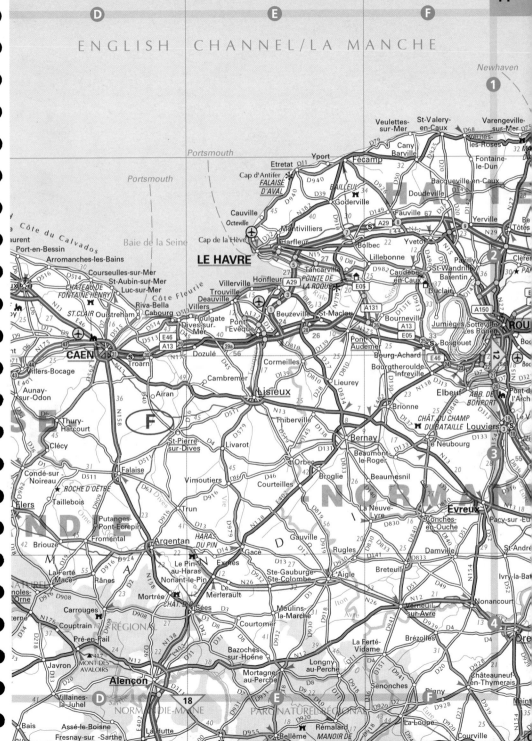

ENGLISH CHANNEL/LA MANCHE

Newhaven

Portsmouth

Portsmouth

Côte du Calvados

Baie de la Seine

Veulettes-sur-Mer
St-Valery-en-Caux
Varengeville-sur-Mer
Veules-les-Roses
Cany Barville
Fontaine-le-Dun
Yport
Fécamp
Etretat
Cap d'Antifer
FALAISE D'AVAL
Goderville
Bacqueville-en-Caux
Doudeville
Fauville
Yerville
Cauville
Octeville
Montivilliers
Bolbec
Yvetot
Cap de la Hève
Harfleur
Lillebonne
Pavilly
St-Wandrille
Barentin
Clères
Tôtes

LE HAVRE

Arromanches-les-Bains
Courseulles-sur-Mer
St-Aubin-sur-Mer
Luc-sur-Mer
Port-en-Bessin
Villerville
Honfleur
POINTE DE LA ROQUE
Caudebec-en-Caux
Duclair
CHÂTEAU DE FONTAINE HENRY
Côte Fleurie
Trouville
Deauville
Riva-Bella
Villers
Cabourg
ST.CLAIR
Ouistreham
Houlgate
Dives-sur-Mer
Pont-l'Évêque
Beuzeville
St-Maclou
Bourneville
Jumièges
Sotteville-lès-Rouen
ROU

CAEN
Troarn
Dozulé
Pont-Audemer
Bourg-Achard
Bourgtheroulde-Infreville
Bosgouet

Villers-Bocage
Cambremer
Cormeilles
Lieurey
Elbeuf
ABB. DE BONPORT
Pont-de-l'Arch

Aunay-sur-Odon
Airan
Lisieux
Thiberville
Brionne
CHÂT. DU CHAMP DU BATAILLE
Louviers
Le V

Thury-Harcourt
F
Bernay
Le Neubourg

Clécy
St-Pierre-sur-Dives
Livarot
Orbec
Beaumont-le-Roger
Beaumesnil

Condé-sur-Noireau
Falaise
Vimoutiers
Courteilles
Broglie
La Neuve-Lyre
Evreux

Taillebois
Trun
Conches-en-Ouche
Pacy-sur-Eu
St-André

Flers
Putanges-Pont-Ecrepin
Fromental
Argentan
HARAS DU PIN
Gauville
Rugles
Damville

Briouze
Exmes
Gacé
Breteuil
Ivry-la-Ba

La Ferté-Macé
Rânes
Le Pin-au-Haras
Nonant-le-Pin
Ste-Gauburge-Ste-Colombe
L'Aigle
Nonancourt

oles-Orne
Mortrée
CHÂT. D
Le Merlerault
Moulins-la-Marche
Verneuil-sur-Avre

Carrouges
Sées
Courtomer
Brézolles
Dre

Couptrain
RÉGIONA
Pré-en-Pail
Bazoches-sur-Hoëne
La Ferté-Vidame

Javron
MONT DES AVALOIRS
Longny-au-Perche
Châteauneuf-en-Thymerais

Alençon
Mortagne-au-Perche
Senonches
La Loupe
Courville

Villaines-la-Juhel
NORMANDIE-MAINE

Bais
Assé-le-Boisne
Fresnay-sur-Sarthe
La Hutte
Mamers
Rémalard
Bellême
MANOIR DE

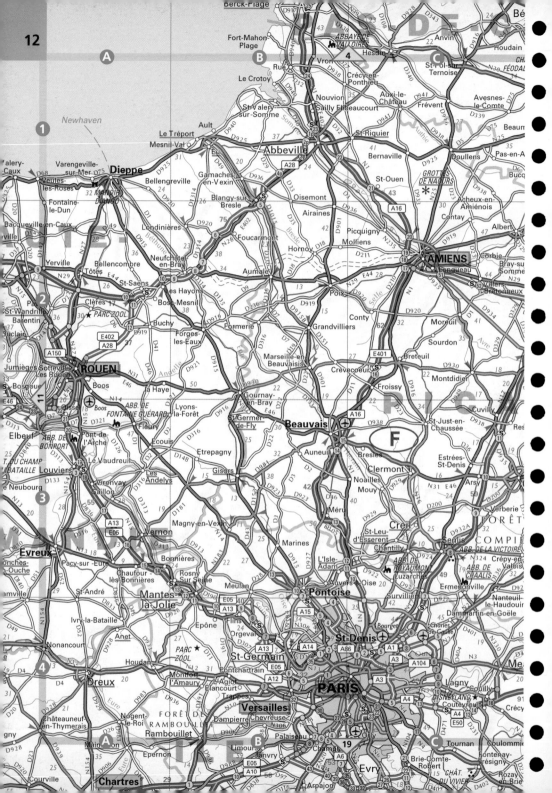

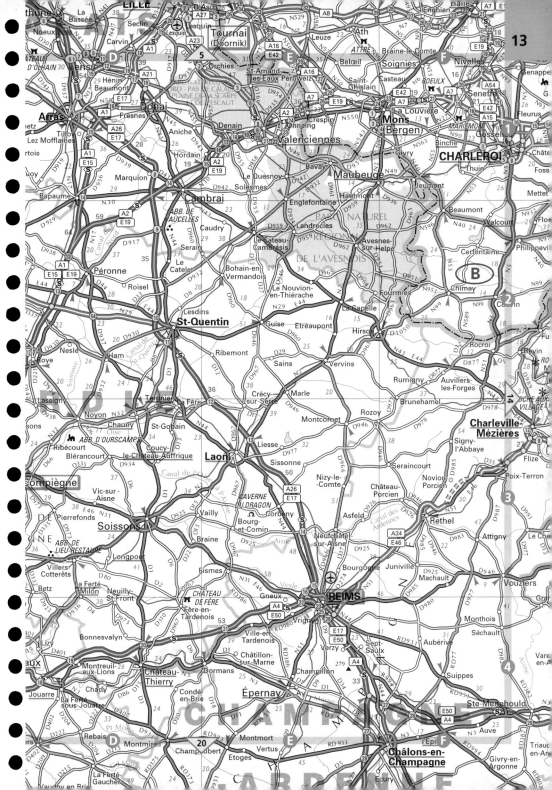

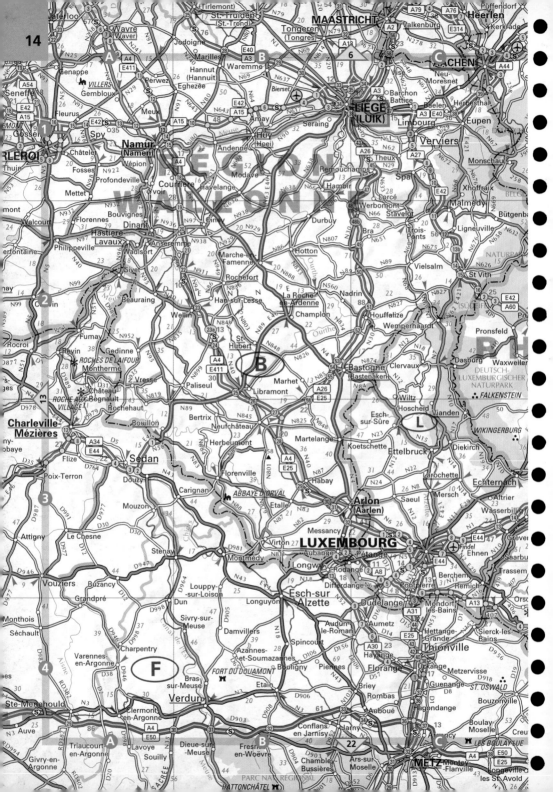

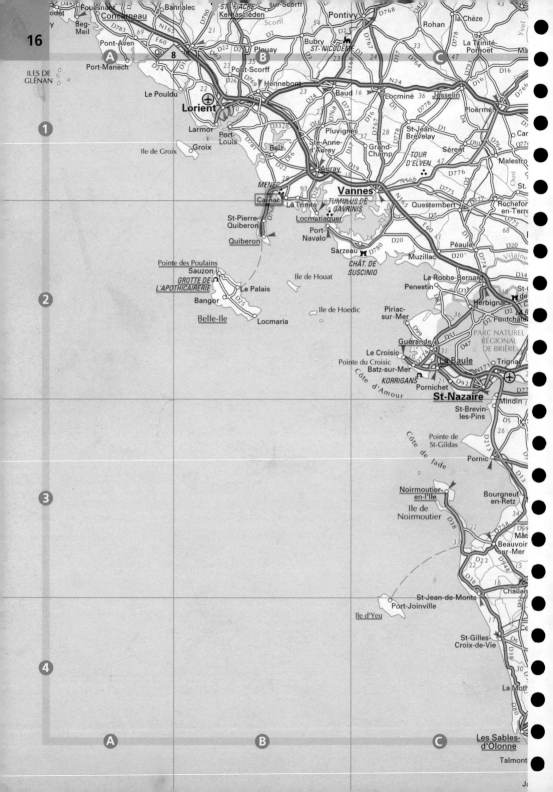

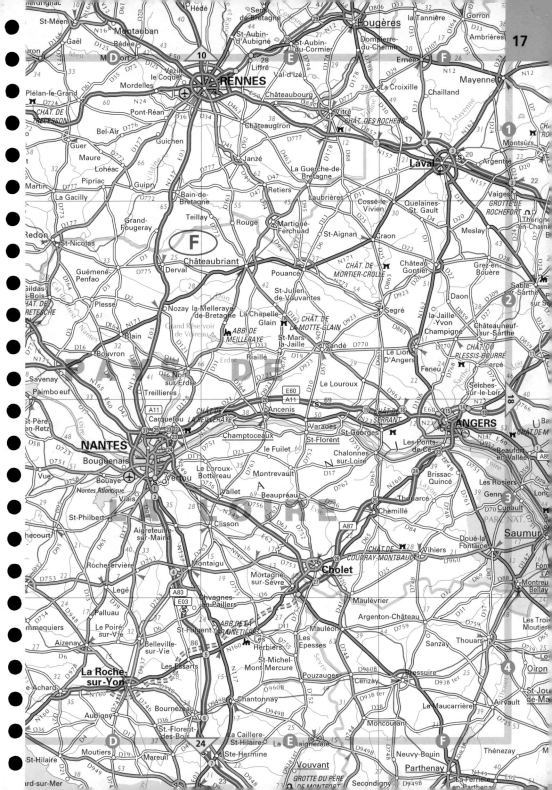

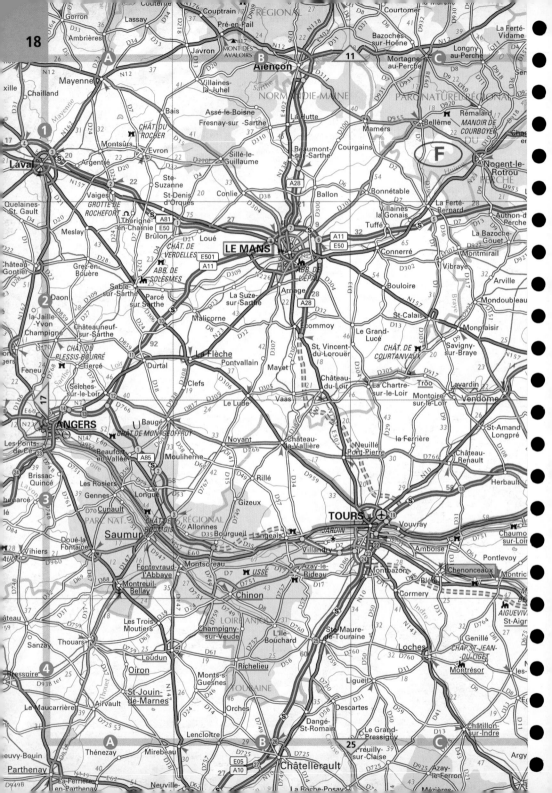

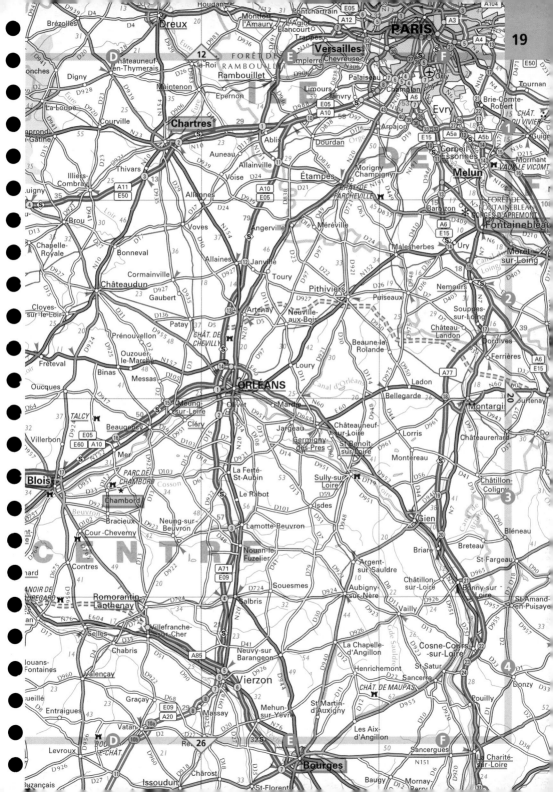

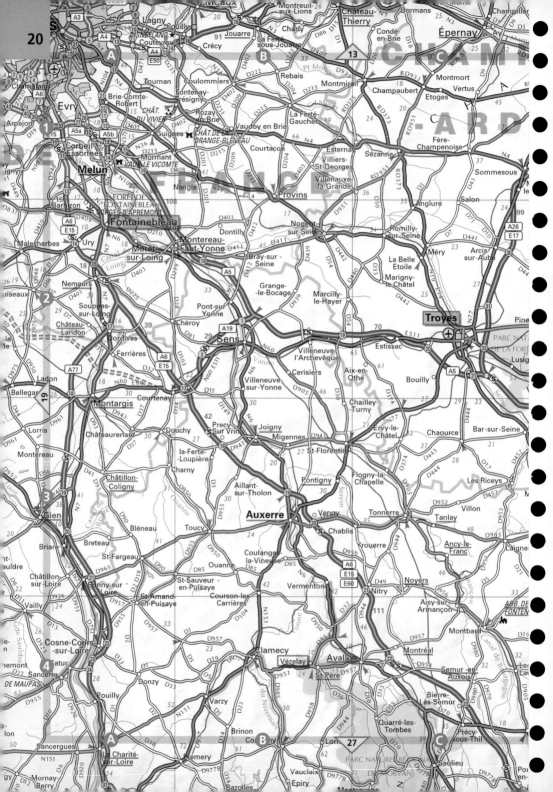

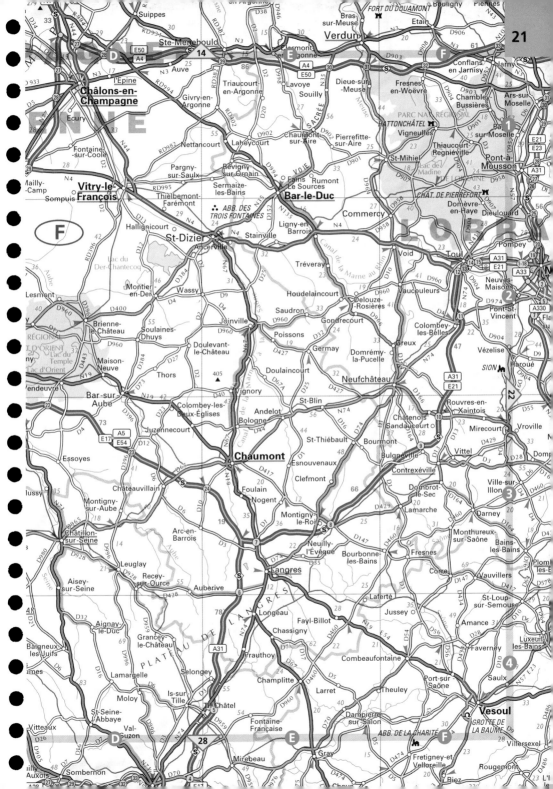

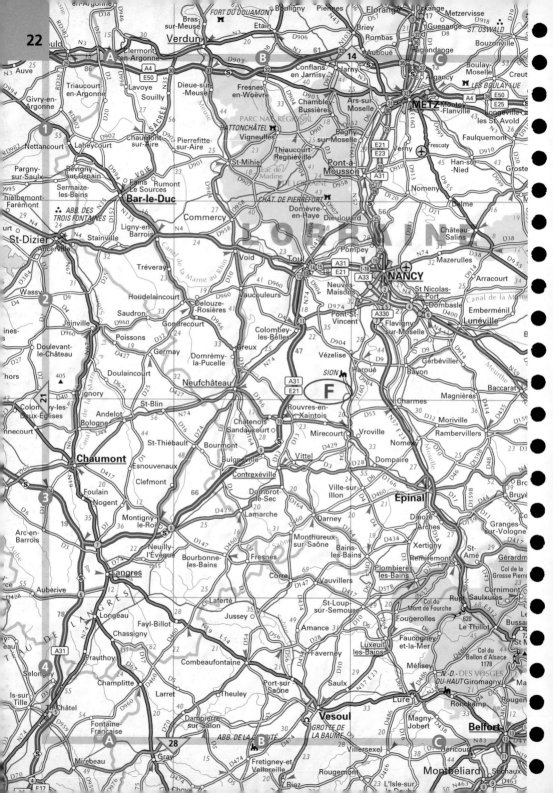

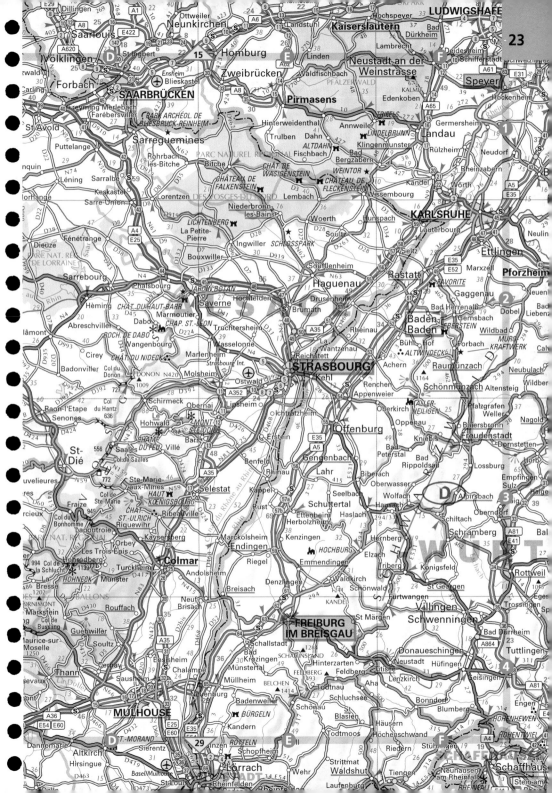

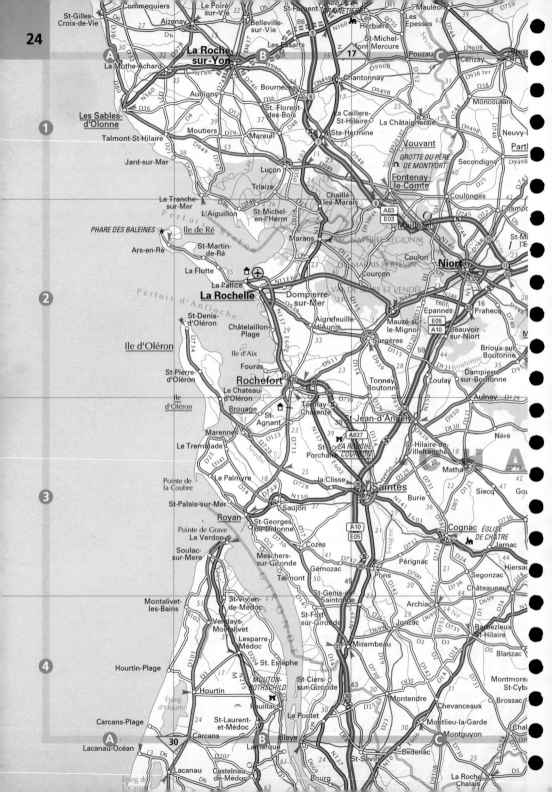

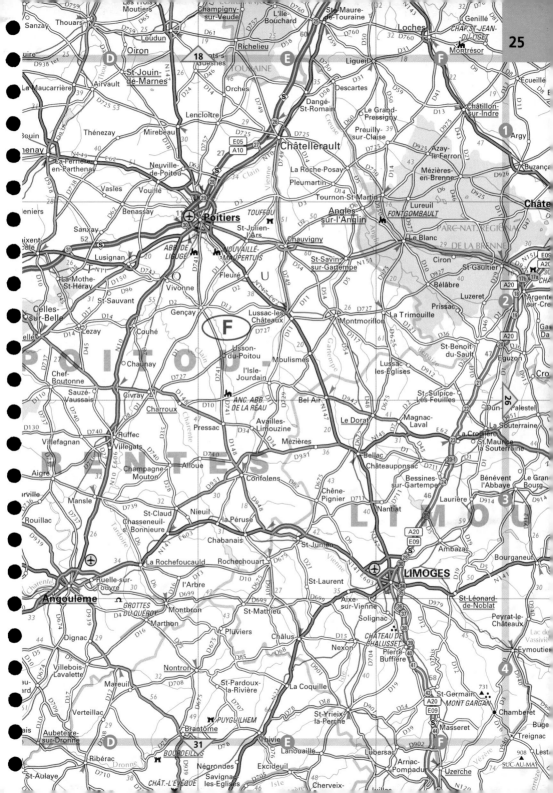

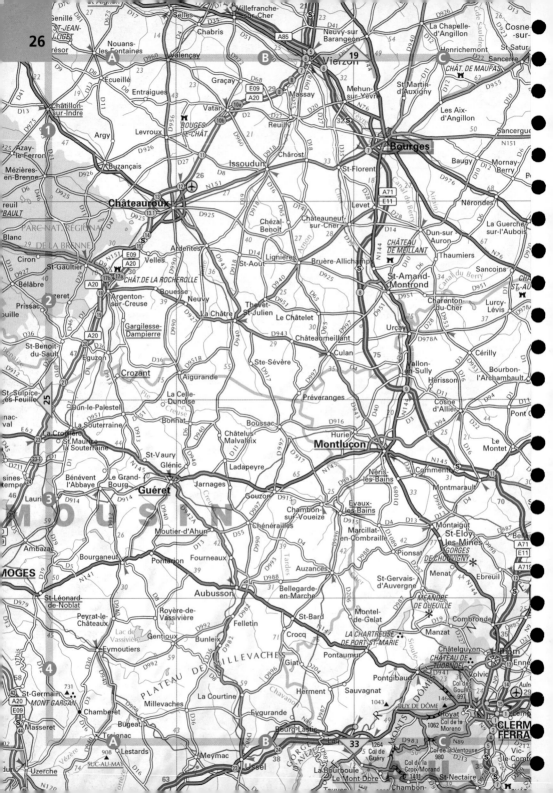

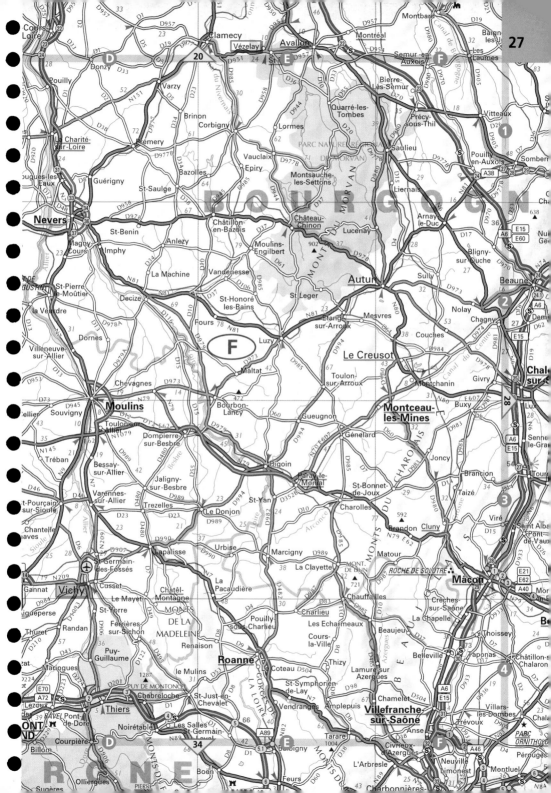

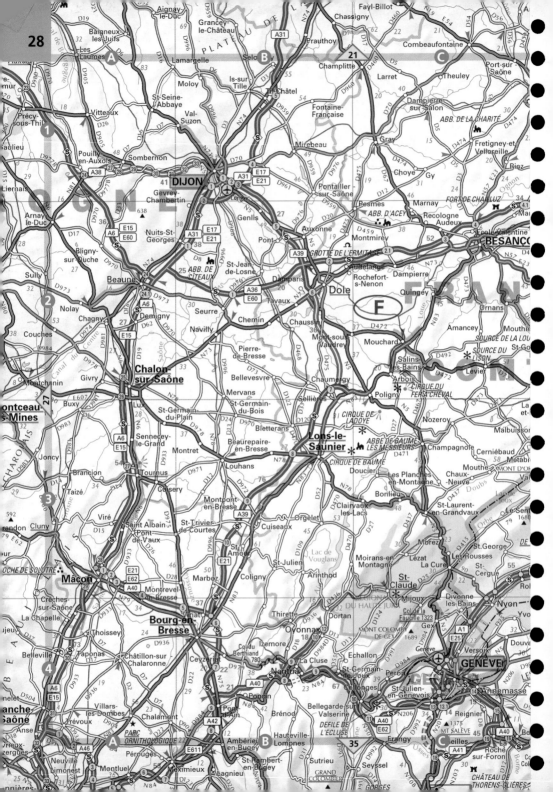

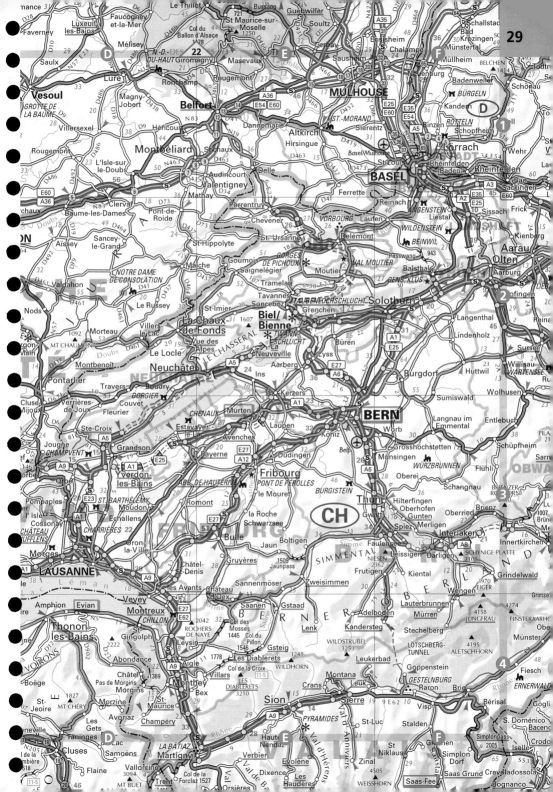

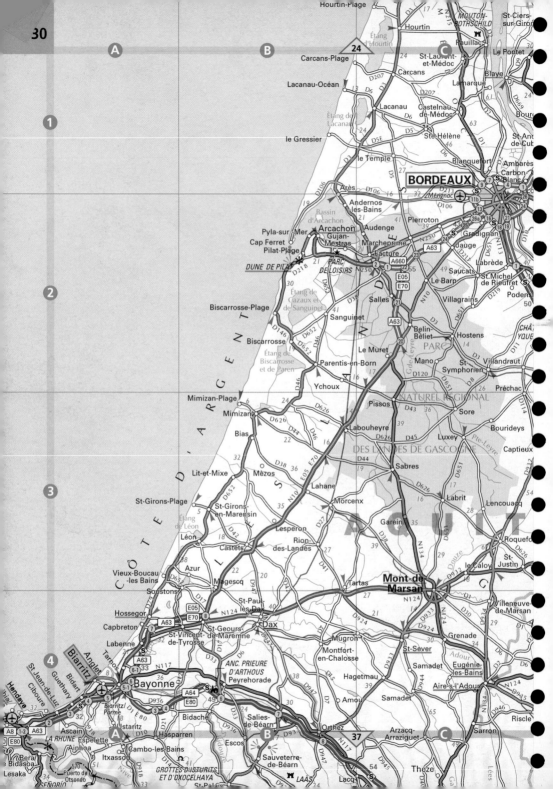

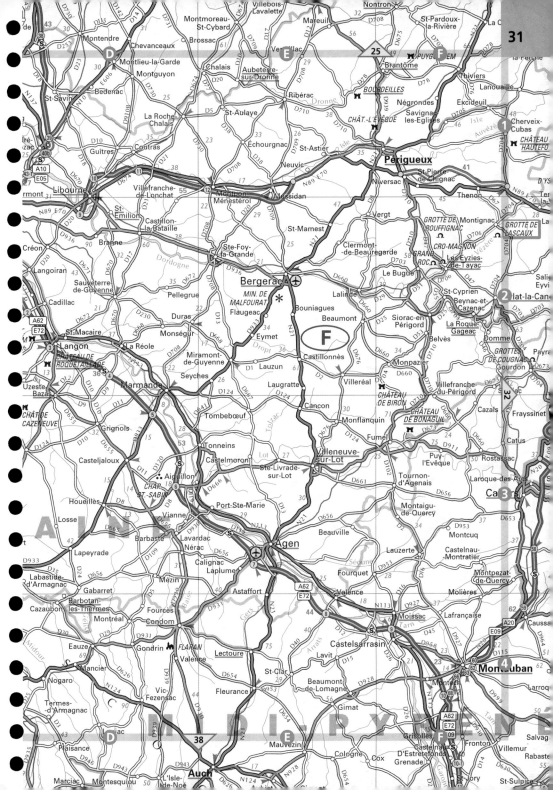

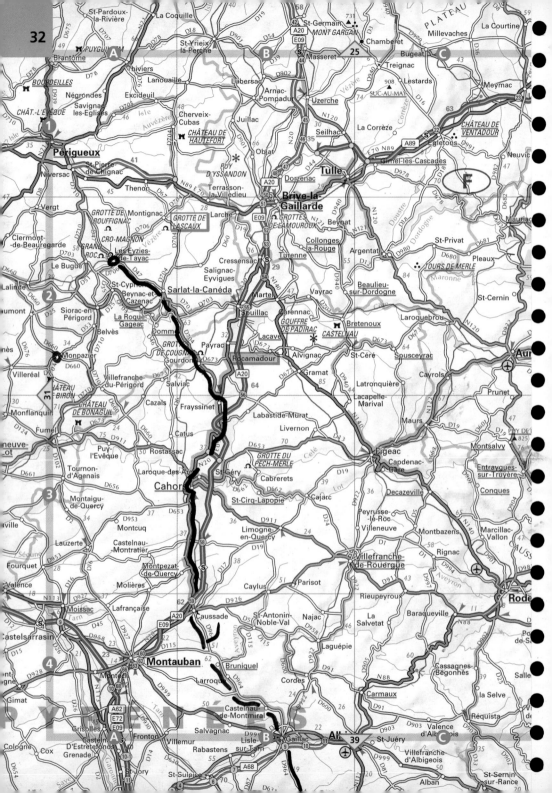

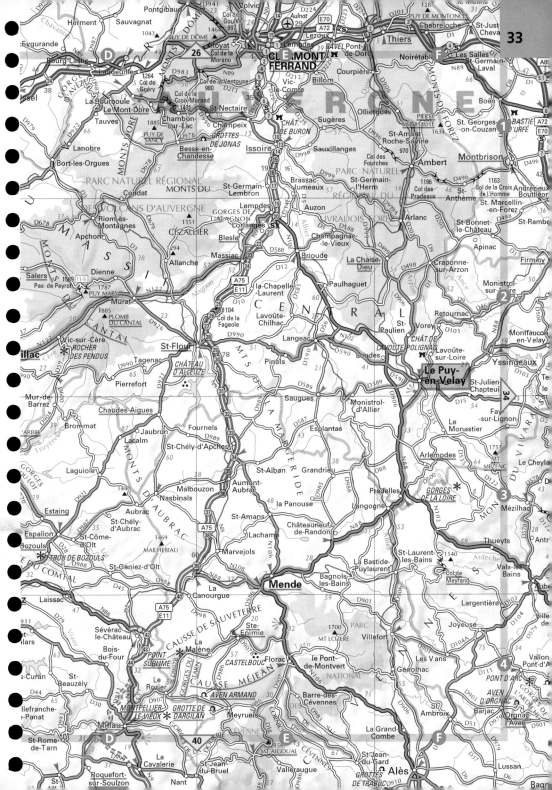

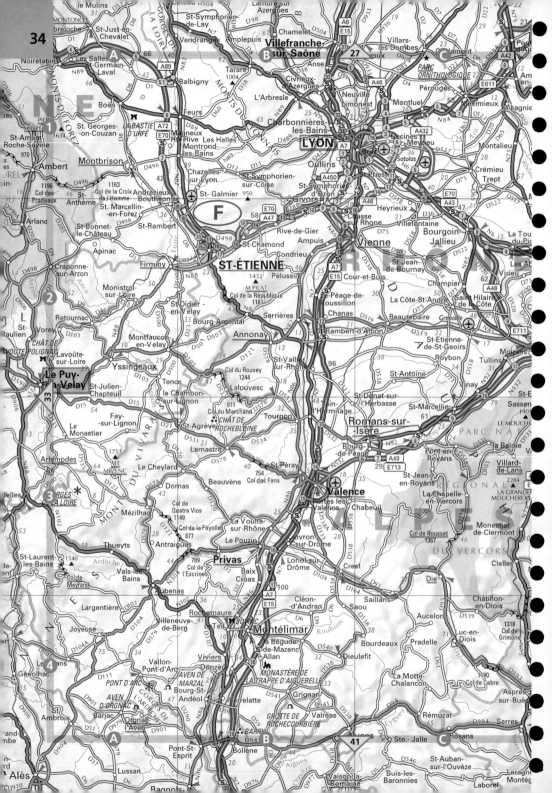

Nantua · Perou · LES VOSGES · Châtel 1369 · Monthey · A9

A40 · St-Germain-de-Joux · St-Julien-en-Genevois · Annemasse · Boège · Pas de Morgins/Morgins · Bex · St-Maurice

Bellegarde-sur-Valserine · Reignier · St-Jeoire · MT CHÉRY 1827 · Morzine · Champéry

Brénod · Collonges · Cellonges · Les Gets · Plan-du-Lac · Avoriaz · LA BÂTIAZ · Martigny · Verb

Hauteville-Lompnes · Frangy · Cruseilles · Bonneville · Faucigny · Cluses · Samoëns · Flaine · Valloreine 3094 · Col de la Forclaz 1527 · Champex · Orsières · Val d'Entremont · Fionna

St-Rambert-en-Bugey · Seyssel · La Roche-sur-Foron · Col de la Colombière 1618 · MT BUET 4807 · Col des Montets 1461 · Trient · GRAND COMBIN

Artemare · Rumilly · ANNECY · Veyrier · Thônes · La Clusaz · Megève · St-Gervais-les-Bains · Sallanches · LE BRÉVENT 2526 · Chamonix-Mont-Blanc · TUNNEL DU MONT-BLANC · Col du Grand-St-Bernard 2473 · Aosta/Aoste · TUNNEL DU ST-BERN

Belley · ABB DE HAUTECOMBE · Albens · Seynod · St-Jorioz · Duingt · Menthon · Talloires · CHÂTEAU DE THORENS-GLIÈRES · CHAINE DES ARAVIS · Col des Aravis 1498 · MT CHARVIN 2407 · Les Houches · Entrèves · Courmayeur · Morgex · Aosta/Aoste

Aix-les-Bains · Le Châtelard · Albertville · Flumet · Ugine · Beaufort-sur-Doron · Pré St-Didier · La Thuile · Col du Petit St-Bernard 2188

Chambéry · Col du Frêne 950 · St-Pierre-d'Albigny · LE GRAND ARC 2489 · Bourg-St-Maurice · Les Arcs · Valgrisenche · RHÊMES N.D. · GRAND PARADISO

Montmélian · Aiguebelle · Aime · St-Marcel · La Plagne · Tignes · Val d'Isère · Col de l'Iseran 2770 · Forno · Ceresole Reale · Alpi Graie

La Rochette · Valmorel · Moûtiers · Bozel · Courchevel · Méribel-les-Allues · Pralognan-la-Vanoise · Val-Claret · ROCHER DE BELLEVARDE 2826 · PARC NATIONAL DE LA VANOISE

Allevard · Col de la Madeleine 1984 · La Chambre · Les Menuires · Val Thorens · Bonneval-sur-Arc · Bessans · CIAMARELLA 3676 · Ala di Stura

Grenoble · Uriage-les-Bains · St-Jean-de-Maurienne · Val Thorens · MASSIF DE LA VANOISE · Col du Glandon 1951 · St-Jeans-d'Arves · St-Michel-de-Maurienne · Lanslebourg-Mont-Cenis · Col du Mont Cenis 2083 · Susa · Bussoleno · Avigli

Chamrousse · Col de la Croix de Fer 2067 · Col du Télégraphe 1570 · Valloire · Modane · ABB. DI NOVALESA · Ussegli · Balme

L'Alpe d'Huez · Le Freney · TUNNEL DE FRÉJUS · ST PIERRE D'EXTRAVACHE · FORTE · Saletta

Le Bourg d'Oisans · Col du Galibier 2645 · MT THABOR 3181 · Bardonécchia · Oulx · Sauze d'Oulx · SACRA DI SAN MICHELE · Rivoli

Vizille · La Grave · Col du Lautaret 2058 · Le Monêtier-les-Bains · La Salle-les-Alpes · Chantemerle · Cesana Torinese · Fenestrelle · Perosa Argentina · Orbassan

La Mure · Les Deux-Alpes · La Bérarde · MASSIF DES ÉCRINS · MT PELVOUX 3914 · Briançon · Colle di Sestriere 2033 · Sestriere · Pinerolo · Perrero · Prali · Piossasco

N.D. DE LA SALETTE · La Chapelle-en-Valgaudemar · Vallouise · L'Argentière-la-Bessée · Montgenèvre · Claviere · Airasca

St-Firmin · PARC NATIONAL DES ÉCRINS · SOMMET DROUVET 3327 · La Roche-de-Rame · Arvieux · Aiguilles · Abriès · Bobbio Pellice · Torre Pellice · Villafran Piémont

Col de la Croix Haute 1176 · St-Bonnet-en-Champsaur · Orcières · St-Clément-sur-Durance · Mt-Dauphin · Château-Queyras · L'Echalp · Bagnolo Piemonte · Barge · Cavour

Lus-la-Croix-Haute · Col Bayard 1248 · St-Véran · Crissolo · Paesana · ABB. DI STAFFARDA · Moretta

St-Julien-en-Beauchêne · GAP · La Bâtie-Neuve · Ceillac · M VISO 3841 · BELVEDERE DU CIRQUE · N.D. DE CLAUSIS · Pontechianale · Casteldelfino · Verzuolo · Salu

Veynes · Chorges · Vars · Embrun · Col de Vars 2109 · Sampèyre · Brossasco · Saluz

Monêtier-Allemont · Savines-le-Lac · St-Vincent-les-Forts · St-Paul · MT CHAMBEYRON 3389 · Stroppo · Busca

La Motte-du-Caire · Le Lauzet-Ubaye · GRAND BÉRARD 3042 · Jausiers · Larche · Col de Larche/Colle della Maddalena 1994 · S. Damiano · Macra · Dronero

ANC. BATTERIE · Seyne · Ubaye · Barcelonnette · Maira · PROVENCE

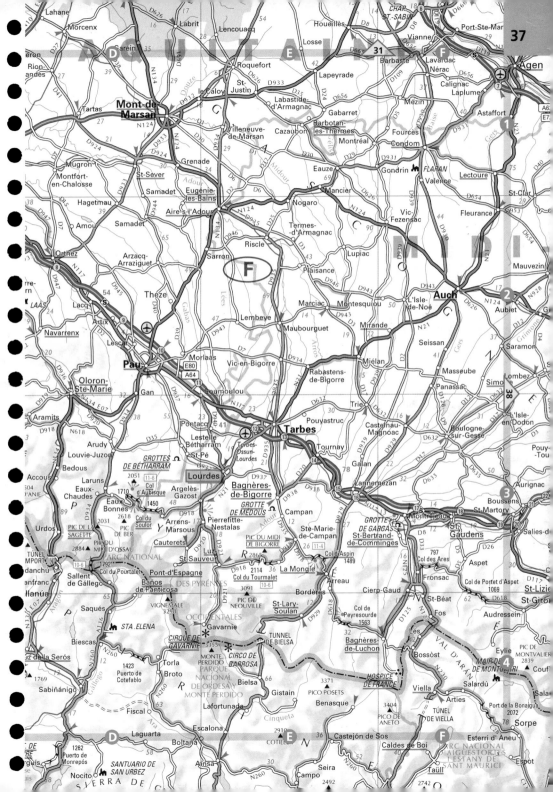

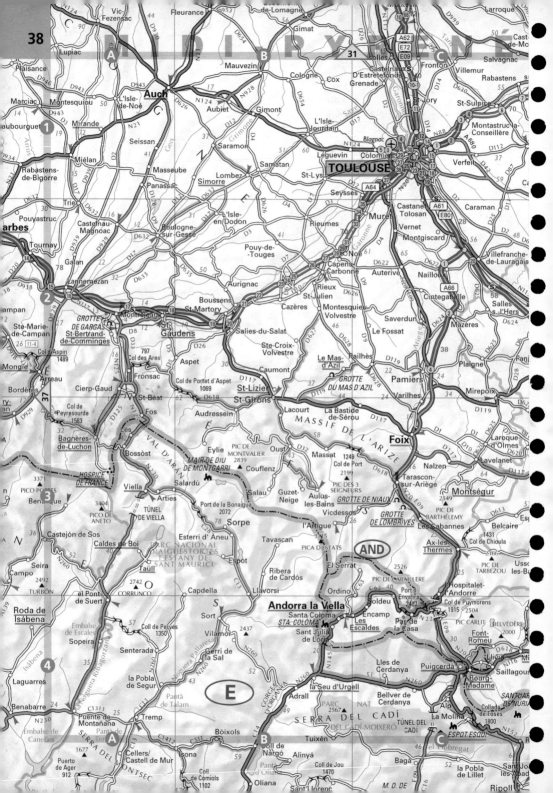

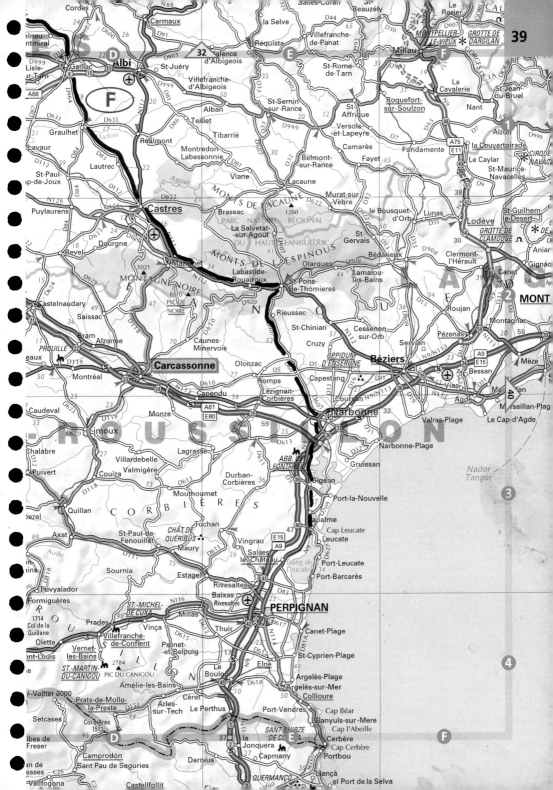

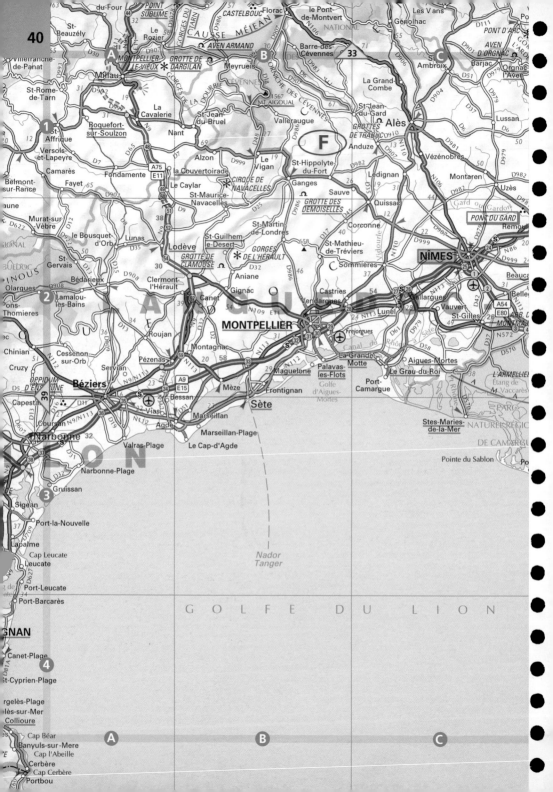

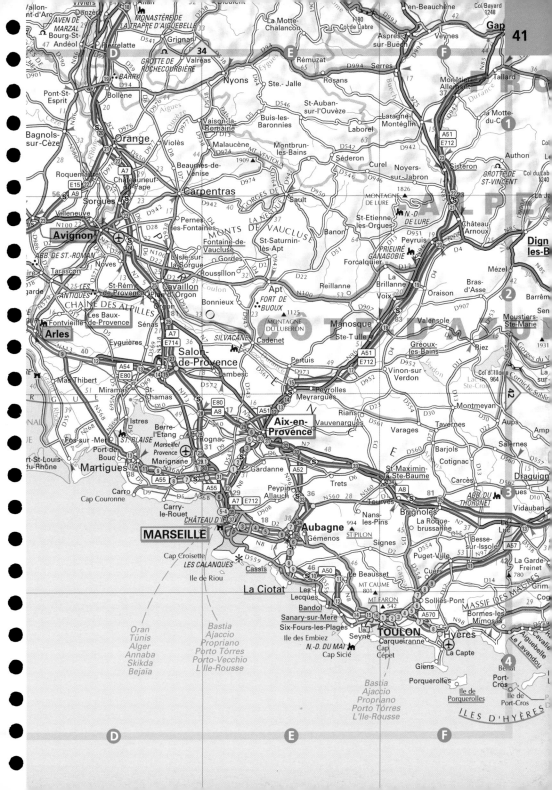

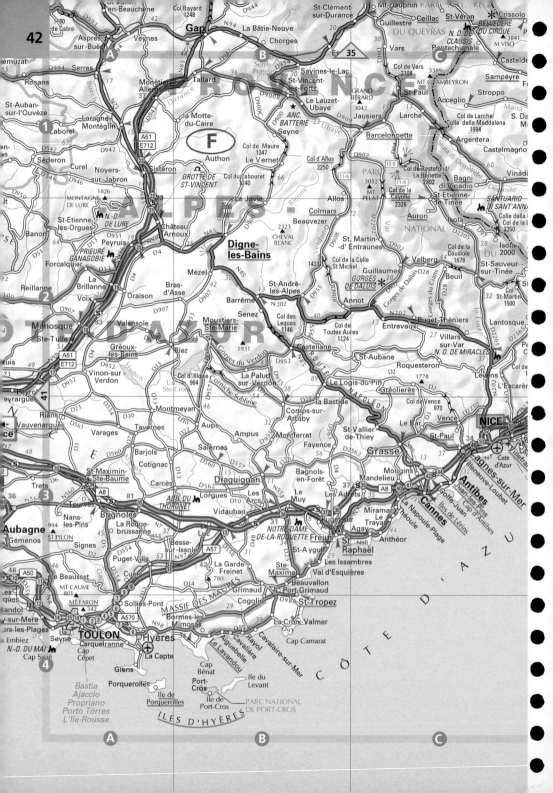

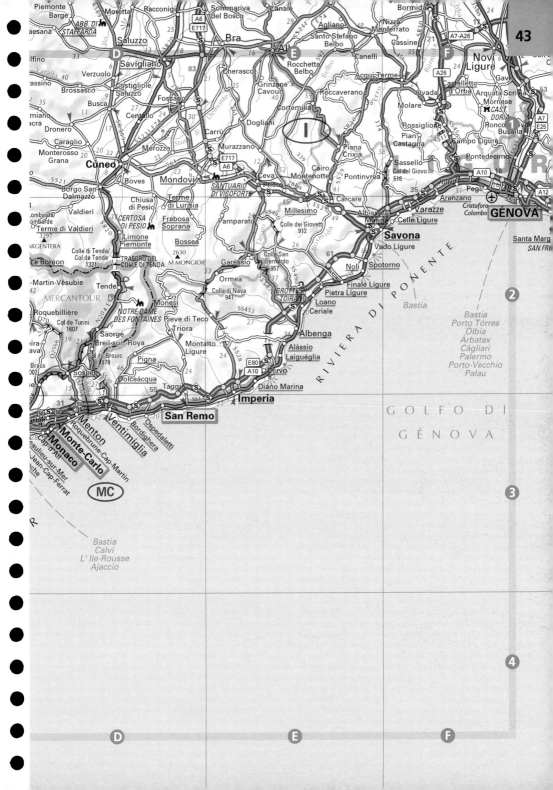

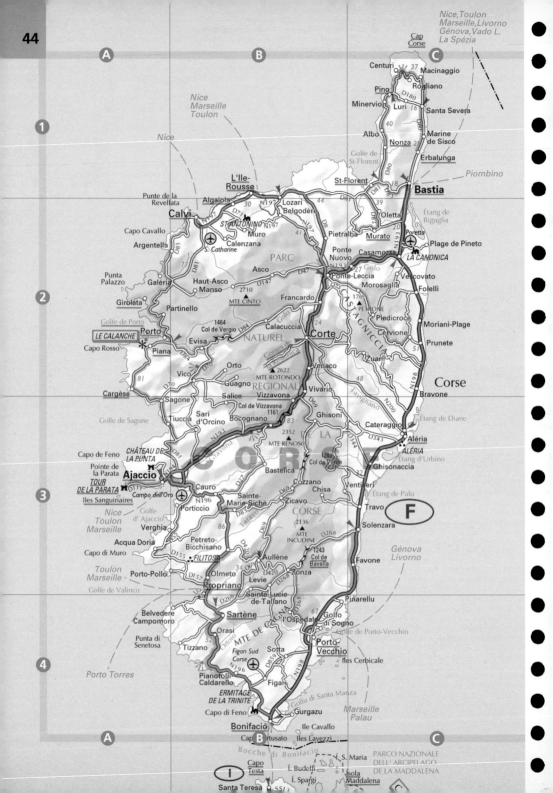

How to use the index
The index lists the place names, tourist sites, main tunnels and passes contained in the atlas, followed by the abbreviation of the country name to which they belong. All names contained in two adjoining pages are referenced to the even page number.

A

Aalburg [NL] 6 B2
Aalsmeer [NL] 2 B4
Aalst (Alost) [B] 4 E4
Aalten [NL] 6 D2
Aalter [B] 4 E3
Aarschot [B] 6 B4
Abbaye d'Orval [B] 14 B3
Abbeville [F] 12 B1
Ablis [F] 18 E1
Abondance [F] 28 D4
Abreschviller [F] 22 D2
Abriès [F] 34 F4
Accous [F] 36 D3

Acey, Abbaye d'– [F] 28 C2
Acheux-en-Amiénois [F] 12 C1
Acqua Doria [F] 44 A3
Afsluitdijk [NL] 2 C2
Agay [F] 42 C3
Agde [F] 38 F3
Agen [F] 30 E3
Agon-Coutainville [F] 10 B2
Ahun [F] 26 B3
Aignay-le-Duc [F] 20 D4
Aigre [F] 24 D3
Aigrefeuille [F] 24 B2
Aigrefeuille-sur-Maine [F] 16 D3
Aiguebelle [F] 42 B4
Aiguebelle [F] 34 E2
Aigueperse [F] 26 C4

Aigues-Mortes [F] 40 C2
Aiguevives [F] 18 C4
Aiguilles [F] 34 E4
Aiguillon [F] 30 D3
Aigurande [F] 26 B2
Ailefroide [F] 34 E3
Aillant-sur-Tholon [F] 20 B3
Aime [F] 34 E2
Ainhoa [F] 36 B2
Airaines [F] 12 B2
Airan [F] 10 D3
Aire [F] 4 C4
Aire-sur-l'Adour [F] 30 C4
Airvault [F] 16 F4
Aisey-sur-Seine [F] 20 D3
Aissey [F] 28 D2
Aisy-sur-Armançon [F] 20 C4

Aix-en-Othe [F] 20 C2
Aix-en-Provence [F] 40 E3
Aixe-sur-Vienne [F] 24 E3
Aix-les-Bains [F] 34 D2
Aizenay [F] 16 D4
Ajaccio [F] 44 A3
Alban [F] 38 E1
Albens [F] 34 D1
Albert [F] 12 C2
Albertville [F] 34 E2
Albi [F] 38 D1
Albo [F] 44 C1
Aldtsier [NL] 2 D2
Alençon [F] 10 D4
Aléria [F] 44 C3
Aléria [F] 44 C3
Alès [F] 40 C1
Algajola [F] 44 B2
Alkmaar [NL] 2 B3
Allaines [F] 18 E2
Allainville [F] 18 E1
Allan [F] 34 B4
Allanche [F] 32 D2
Allauch [F] 40 E3
Allemont [F] 34 D3

Alleuze, Château d'– [F] 32 D2
Allevard [F] 34 D2
Allonnes [F] 18 B3
Allonnes [F] 18 E2
Allos [F] 42 B1
Alloue [F] 24 E3
Almelo [NL] 2 E4
Almere [NL] 2 C4
Alost (Aalst) [B] 4 E4
Alphen-aan den Rijn [NL] 2 B4
Altkirch [F] 28 E1
Altrier [L] 14 C3
Alvignac [F] 32 B2
Alzon [F] 40 B1
Alzonne [F] 38 D2
Amance [F] 20 F4
Amancey [F] 28 C2
Amay [B] 14 B1
Ambarès [F] 30 D1
Ambazac [F] 24 F3
Ambérieu-en-Bugey [F] 34 C1
Ambert [F] 32 F1

Amboise [F] 18 C3
Ambrières [F] 10 C4
Amélie-les-Bains [F] 38 D4
Amerongen [NL] 6 C2
Amersfoort [NL] 2 C4
Amiens [F] 12 C2
Amou [F] 30 B4
Amphion [F] 28 D4
Amplepuis [F] 26 E4
Ampuis [F] 34 B2
Ampus [F] 42 B3
Amsterdam [NL] 2 B3
Ancenis [F] 16 E3
Ancerville [F] 20 E2
Ancy-le-Franc [F] 20 C3
Andelot [F] 20 E3
Andenne [B] 14 B1
Andernos-les-Bains [F] 30 B2
Andijk [NL] 2 C3
Andolsheim [F] 22 D3
Andrézieux-Bouthéon [F] 34 A2
Anduze [F] 40 C1
Anet [F] 12 A4
Angers [F] 16 F3
Angerville [F] 18 E2
Angles-sur-l'Anglin [F] 24 E2
Anglet [F] 30 A4
Anglure [F] 20 C2
Ango, Manoir d'- [F] 12 A1
Angoulême [F] 24 D3
Aniane [F] 40 B2
Aniche [F] 12 D1
Anjum [NL] 2 D2
Anlezy [F] 26 D2
Anna Paulowna [NL] 2 B2
Annecy [F] 34 E1
Annemasse [F] 28 C4
Annonay [F] 34 B2
Annot [F] 42 B2
Anse [F] 26 F4
Anseremme [F] 14 A2
Anthéor [F] 42 C3
Antibes [F] 42 C3
Antraigues [F] 34 A3
Antrain [F] 8 F4
Antwerpen (Anvers) [B] 4 F3
Anvers (Antwerpen) [B] 4 F3
Apchon [F] 32 D2
Apeldoorn [NL] 2 D4
Apinac [F] 32 F2
Apothicairerie, Grotte de l'- [F] 16 B2
Appingedam [NL] 2 E2
Apremont, Gorges d'- [F] 18 F2
Apt [F] 40 E2
Aramits [F] 36 D3
Arbois [F] 28 C2
Arc, Pont d'- [F] 34 A4
Arcachon [F] 30 B2
Arcen [F] 6 D3
Arc-en-Barrois [F] 20 D3
Arches [F] 22 C3
Archiac [F] 24 C4
Arcis-sur-Aube [F] 20 C2
Ardentes [F] 26 B1
Ardres [F] 4 B4
Arendonk [B] 6 B3
Arès [F] 30 B2
Argancy [F] 14 C4
Argelès-Gazost [F] 36 E3
Argelès-Plage [F] 38 E4
Argelès-sur-Mer [F] 38 E4
Argentan [F] 10 D3
Argentat [F] 32 C2
Argentella [F] 44 B2
Argentière [F] 34 F1
Argenton-Château [F] 16 F4

Argenton-sur-Creuse [F] 26 A2
Argentré [F] 16 F1
Argent-sur-Sauldre [F] 18 E3
Argy [F] 26 A1
Arinthod [F] 28 B3
Arlanc [F] 32 F2
Arlempdes [F] 32 F3
Arles [F] 40 D2
Arles-sur-Tech [F] 38 D4
Arlon [B] 14 B3
Armentières [F] 4 D4
Arnac-Pompadur [F] 32 B1
Arnage [F] 18 B2
Arnay-le-Duc [F] 26 F2
Arnhem [NL] 6 C2
Arpajon [F] 18 E1
Arracourt [F] 22 C2
Arras [F] 12 D1
Arreau [F] 36 E3
Arrens-Marsous [F] 36 D3
Arromanches-les-Bains [F] 10 D2
Ars-en-Ré [F] 24 A2
Ars-sur-Moselle [F] 22 C1
Arsy [F] 12 C3
Artemare [F] 34 D1
Artenay [F] 18 E2
Arthous, Ancient Prieure d'- [F] 30 B4
Artix [F] 36 D2
Arudy [F] 36 D3
Arvieux [F] 34 E4
Arville [F] 18 C2
Arzacq-Arraziguet [F] 36 D2
As [B] 6 C4
Ascain [F] 30 A4
Asco [F] 44 B2
Asfeld [F] 12 E3
Aspet [F] 36 F3
Aspres-sur-Buëch [F] 34 D4
Assé-le-Boisne [F] 18 B1
Assen [NL] 2 E2
Astaffort [F] 30 E4
Asten [NL] 6 C3
Attigny [F] 12 F3
Aubagne [F] 40 E3
Aubange [B] 14 B3
Aubenas [F] 34 A3
Auberive [F] 20 D3
Aubérive [F] 12 F4
Aubeterre-sur-Dronne [F] 30 E1
Aubiet [F] 38 E1
Aubigny [F] 16 D4
Aubigny-sur-Nere [F] 18 E3
Aboué [F] 14 C4
Aubrac [F] 32 D3
Aubusson [F] 26 B3
Aucelon [F] 34 C4
Auch [F] 36 F2
Audelange [F] 28 B2
Audenge [F] 30 C2
Auderville [F] 8 F1
Audeux [F] 28 C2
Audierne [F] 8 A3
Audincourt [F] 28 E1
Audressein [F] 38 B3
Audruicq [F] 4 B4
Audun-le-Roman [F] 14 C4
Aullène [F] 44 B3
Aulnay [F] 24 C3
Ault [F] 12 B1
Aulus-les-Bains [F] 38 B3
Aumale [F] 12 B2
Aumetz [F] 14 C4
Aumont-Aubrac [F] 32 E3
Aunay-sur-Odon [F] 10 D3
Auneau [F] 18 E1
Auneuil [F] 12 B3
Aups [F] 40 F3

Auray [F] 16 B1
Aurignac [F] 38 B2
Aurillac [F] 32 C2
Auron [F] 42 C2
Auterive [F] 38 C2
Authon [F] 42 B1
Authon-du-Perche [F] 18 C2
Autun [F] 26 F2
Auve [F] 12 F4
Auvers-s-Oise [F] 12 B3
Auvillers-les-Forges [F] 12 F2
Auxerre [F] 20 B3
Auxi-le-Château [F] 12 C1
Auxonne [F] 28 B2
Auzances [F] 26 B3
Auzon [F] 32 E2
Availles-Limouzine [F] 24 E3
Aval, Falaise d'- [F] 10 E2
Avallon [F] 20 C4
Aven Armand [F] 32 E4
Aven de Marzal [F] 34 A4
Aven d'Orgnac [F] 34 A4
Averbode [B] 6 B4
Avesnes-le-Comte [F] 12 C1
Avesnes-sur-Helpe [F] 12 E2
Avignon [F] 40 D2
Avoriaz [F] 28 D4
Avranches [F] 10 B3
Axat [F] 38 D3
Axel [NL] 4 E3
Ax-les-Thermes [F] 38 C3
Ay [F] 12 E4
Azannes-et-Soumazannes [F] 14 B4
Azay-le-Ferron [F] 24 F1
Azay-le-Rideau [F] 18 B3
Azur [F] 30 B3

B

Baarle Nassau [NL] 6 B3
Baarn [NL] 2 C4
Baccarat [F] 22 D2
Bacqueville-en-Caux [F] 12 A2
Badonviller [F] 22 D2
Bagnères-de-Bigorre [F] 36 E3
Bagnères-de-Luchon [F] 36 F4
Bagnoles-de-l'Orne [F] 10 D4
Bagnols-en-Forêt [F] 42 B3
Bagnols-les-Bains [F] 32 E3
Bagnols-sur-Cèze [F] 40 D1
Baigneux-les-Juifs [F] 20 D4
Bailleul [F] 4 C4
Bailleul [F] 10 E2
Bain-de-Bretagne [F] 16 D1
Bains-les-Bains [F] 22 C3
Bais [F] 18 A1
Baix [F] 34 B3
Baixas [F] 38 E4
Balbigny [F] 34 A1
Baleines, Phare des- [F] 24 A2
Balleroy [F] 10 C2
Ballon [F] 18 B1
Bandol [F] 40 E4
Bangor [F] 16 B2
Bannalec [F] 8 C4
Banon [F] 40 E2
Banyuls-sur-Mer [F] 38 E4
Bapaume [F] 12 D1
Baraqueville [F] 32 C4

Barbaste [F] 30 D3
Barbezieux [F] 24 C4
Barbizon [F] 18 F2
Barbotan-les-Thermes [F] 30 D4
Barcelonnette [F] 42 C1
Barentin [F] 10 F2
Barenton [F] 10 C3
Barfleur [F] 10 C1
Barjac [F] 34 A4
Barjols [F] 40 F3
Bar-le-Duc [F] 20 E1
Barneveld [NL] 2 C4
Barneville-Carteret [F] 10 B2
Barr [F] 22 D3
Barre-des-Cévennes [F] 32 E4
Barrême [F] 42 B2
Barry [F] 34 B4
Bar-sur-Aube [F] 20 D2
Bar-sur-Seine [F] 20 C3
Bastelica [F] 44 B3
Bastia [F] 44 C1
Bastogne [B] 14 B2
Battice [B] 14 C1
Batz-sur-Mer [F] 16 C2
Baud [F] 16 B1
Baugé [F] 18 A3
Baugy [F] 26 C1
Baume, Cirque de- [F] 28 B3
Baume, Grotte de la- [F] 20 F4
Baume-les-Dames [F] 28 D2
Baume-Les Messiers, Abbaye de- [F] 28 C3
Bavay [F] 12 E1
Bayard [F] 34 B4
Bayeux [F] 10 D2
Bayon [F] 22 C2
Bayonne [F] 30 A4
Bazas [F] 30 D2
Bazoches-sur-Hoëne [F] 10 E4
Bazolles [F] 26 E1
Beaucaire [F] 40 D2
Beaufort-en-Vallée [F] 18 A3
Beaufort-sur-Doron [F] 34 E2
Beaugency [F] 18 D3
Beaujeu [F] 26 F4
Beaulieu-sur-Dordogne [F] 32 B2
Beaulieu-sur-Mer [F] 42 C3
Beaumes de Venise [F] 40 D1
Beaumesnil [F] 10 F3
Beaumetz [F] 12 D1
Beaumont [B] 12 F2
Beaumont [F] 30 E2
Beaumont [F] 10 B1
Beaumont-de-Lomagne [F] 30 E4
Beaumont-le-Roger [F] 10 F3
Beaumont-sur-Sarthe [F] 18 B1
Beaune [F] 28 A2
Beaune-la-Rolande [F] 18 F2
Beaupréau [F] 16 E3
Beauraing [B] 14 A2
Beauregard, Manoir de- [F] 18 D4
Beaurepaire [F] 34 C2
Beaurepaire-en-Bresse [F] 28 B3
Beauvais [F] 12 B3
Beauvallon [F] 42 B3
Beauvène [F] 34 B3
Beauvezer [F] 42 B2
Beauville [F] 30 E3
Beauvoir-sur-Mer [F] 16 C3
Beauvoir-sur-Niort [F] 24 C2

Bécherel [F] 8 E4
Bédarieux [F] 38 F2
Bédée [F] 8 E4
Bedenac [F] 30 D1
Bedous [F] 36 D3
Beek [NL] 6 C4
Beek en Donk [NL] 6 C3
Bégard [F] 8 D3
Beg-Meil [F] 8 B4
Beilen [NL] 2 E3
Bélâbre [F] 24 F2
Bel Air [F] 24 E2
Bel-Air [F] 16 D1
Belcaire [F] 38 C3
Belfort [F] 22 C4
Belgodère [F] 44 B2
Belin-Béliet [F] 30 C2
Bellac [F] 24 E3
Bellegarde [F] 18 F2
Bellegarde [F] 40 C2
Bellegarde-en-Marche [F] 26 B3
Bellegarde-sur-Valserine [F] 28 C4
Belle-Isle-en-Terre [F] 8 C3
Bellême [F] 18 C1
Bellenaves [F] 26 C3
Bellencombre [F] 12 A2
Bellengreville [F] 12 A1
Bellesvre [F] 28 B2
Belleville [F] 26 F4
Belleville-sur-Vie [F] 16 D4
Belley [F] 34 D1
Belmont-sur-Rance [F] 38 E1
Beloeil [B] 12 E1
Belvedere Campomoro [F] 44 B4
Belvedere du Cirque [F] 34 F4
Belvès [F] 30 F2
Belz [F] 16 B1
Benassay [F] 24 D2
Bénévent l'Abbaye [F] 26 A3
Benfeld [F] 22 E3
Bénodet [F] 8 B4
Berchem [L] 14 C3
Bergen [NL] 2 B3
Bergen (Mons) [B] 12 F1
Bergen aan Zee [NL] 2 B3
Bergen op Zoom [NL] 4 F3
Bergerac [F] 30 E2
Bergues [F] 4 C3
Bergum [NL] 2 D2
Beringen [B] 6 B4
Bernaville [F] 12 C1
Bernay [F] 10 E3
Berre-l'Etang [F] 40 D3
Bertrix [B] 14 B3
Besançon [F] 28 C2
Bessan [F] 38 F2
Bessans [F] 34 F3
Bessay-sur-Allier [F] 26 D3
Besse-en-Chandesse [F] 32 D1
Besse-sur-Issole [F] 40 F3
Bessines-sur-Gartempe [F] 24 F3
Bétharram, Grottes de- [F] 36 D3
Betz [F] 12 D3
Beuil [F] 42 C2
Beuzeville [F] 10 E2
Beveren-Waas [B] 4 F3
Beverwijk [NL] 2 B3
Beynac-et-Cazenac [F] 30 F2
Beynat [F] 32 B2
Béziers [F] 38 F2
Biarritz [F] 30 A4
Bias [F] 30 B3
Bidache [F] 30 B4

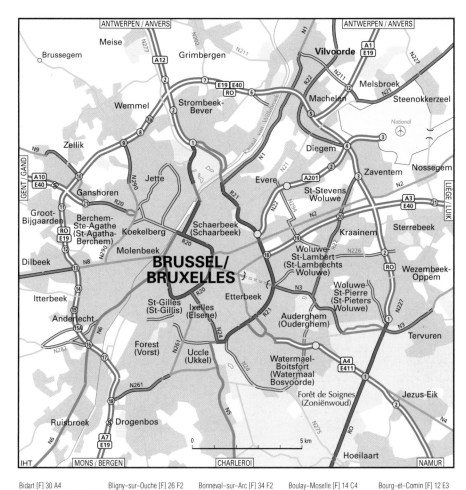

Bidart [F] 30 A4
Bierre-Lès-Semur [F] 20 C4
Billom [F] 32 E1
Binas [F] 18 D2
Binche [B] 12 F1
Binic [F] 8 D3
Biron, Château de– [F] 30 F2
Biscarrosse [F] 30 B2
Biscarrosse–Plage [F] 30 B2
Bitche [F] 22 E1
Blain [F] 16 D2
Blâmont [F] 22 D2
Blangy-sur-Bresle [F] 12 B1
Blankenberge [B] 4 D3
Blanquefort [F] 30 C1
Blanzac [F] 24 C4
Blaye [F] 30 C1
Bléneau [F] 20 A3
Blérancourt [F] 12 D3
Bléré [F] 18 C3
Blériot–Plage [F] 4 B3
Blesle [F] 32 E2
Bletterans [F] 28 B3
Bliesbruck–Reinheim, Parc
  Archéol. de– [F] 22 D1

Bligny-sur-Ouche [F] 26 F2
Blois [F] 18 D3
Blokzijl [NL] 2 D3
Bocholt [B] 6 C4
Bocognano [F] 44 B3
Bodegraven [NL] 2 B4
Boëge [F] 28 C4
Boën [F] 34 A1
Bohain–en–Vermandois [F]
  12 E2
Bois–du–Four [F] 32 D4
Bolbec [F] 10 E2
Bollène [F] 40 D1
Bologne [F] 20 E3
Bolsward [NL] 2 C2
Bonaguil, Château de– [F] 30
  32 F1
Bonhomme, Col du– [F] 22
  D3
Bonifacio [F] 44 B4
Bonlieu [F] 28 C3
Bonnat [F] 26 B3
Bonnesvalyn [F] 12 D4
Bonnétable [F] 18 C1
Bonneval [F] 18 D2

Bonneval-sur-Arc [F] 34 F2
Bonneville [F] 28 C4
Bonnières [F] 12 A3
Bonnieux [F] 40 E2
Bonny-sur-Loire [F] 18 F3
Bonport, Abbaye de– [F] 12
  A3
Boom [B] 4 F4
Boos [F] 12 A2
Borculo [NL] 6 D2
Bordeaux [F] 30 C2
Bordères [F] 36 E3
Borger [NL] 2 E3
Bormes–les–Mimosas [F] 42
  B4
Bort–les–Orgues [F]
  32 D1
Boskoop [NL] 2 B4
Bouaye [F] 16 D3
Bouesse [F] 26 A2
Bouges–Le–Château [F] 18
  D4
Bouguenais [F] 16 D3
Bouillon [B] 14 A3
Bouilly [F] 20 C2

Boulay–Moselle [F] 14 C4
Bouligny [F] 14 B4
Boulogne [F] 4 B4
Boulogne–sur–Gesse [F] 36
  F3
Bouloire [F] 18 C2
Boumois, Château de– [F] 18
  A3
Bouniagues [F] 30 E2
Bourbon-Lancy [F] 26 E2
Bourbon–l'Archambault [F]
  26 C2
Bourbonne–les–Bains [F] 20
  F3
Bourbourg [F] 4 C3
Bourbriac [F] 8 D3
Bourdeaux [F] 34 C4
Bourdeilles [F] 30 E1
Bourg [F] 30 D1
Bourg–Achard [F] 10 F2
Bourganeuf [F] 26 A3
Bourg–Argental [F] 34 B2
Bourg–de–Péage [F] 34 C4
Bourg–en–Bresse [F] 28 B4
Bourges [F] 26 C1

Bourg–et–Comin [F] 12 E3
Bourg–Lastic [F] 26 B4
Bourg–Madame [F] 38 C4
Bourgneuf–en–Retz [F] 16 D3
Bourgogne [F] 12 E3
Bourgoin-Jallieu [F] 34 C2
Bourg–St–Andéol [F] 34 B4
Bourg–St–Maurice [F] 34 E2
Bourgtheroulde–Infreville [F]
  10 F3
Bourgueil [F] 18 B3
Bourideys [F] 30 C3
Bourmont [F] 20 E3
Bourneville [F] 10 F2
Bournezeau [F] 16 D4
Boussac [F] 26 B3
Boussens [F] 38 B2
Bouvignes [B] 14 A2
Bouvron [F] 16 D2
Bouxwiller [F] 22 E2
Bouzonville [F] 14 C4
Boxmeer [NL] 6 C3
Boxtel [NL] 6 B3
Bozel [F] 34 E2
Bozouls [F] 32 D3

Bozouls, Trou de– [F] 32 D3
Bra [B] 14 C2
Bracieux [F] 18 D3
Braine [F] 12 D3
Brakel [B] 4 E4
Bram [F] 38 D2
Brancion [F] 26 F3
Brandon [F] 26 F3
Branne [F] 30 D2
Brantôme [F] 24 D4
Bras–d'Asse [F] 40 F2
Brassac [F] 38 C2
Brassac-les-Mines [F] 32 E1
Brasschaat [B] 4 F3
Bras–sur–Meuse [F] 14 B4
Braus, Col de– [F] 42 D2
Bravone [F] 44 C2
Bray–sur–Seine [F] 20 B2
Bray–sur–Somme [F] 12 D2
Brécey [F] 10 C3
Brecht [B] 6 A3
Breda [NL] 6 B3
Bree [B] 6 C4
Bréhal [F] 10 B3
Breil-sur-Roya [F] 42 D2
Brénod [F] 28 B4
Breskens [NL] 4 E3
Bresles [F] 12 C3
Bressuire [F] 16 F4
Brest [F] 8 B3
Breteau [F] 18 F3
Bretenoux [F] 32 B2
Bretesche, Château de la– [F] 16 C2
Breteuil [F] 12 C2
Breteuil [F] 10 F4
Brézolles [F] 10 F4
Briançon [F] 34 E3
Briare [F] 18 F3
Bricquebec [F] 10 B1
Briec [F] 8 B3
Brie–Comte–Robert [F] 18 F1
Brielle [NL] 4 F2
Brienne–le–Château [F] 20 D2
Briey [F] 14 C4
Brignogan–Plage [F] 8 B2
Brignoles [F] 40 F3
Brignoud [F] 34 D2
Brinon [F] 20 B4
Brionne [F] 10 F3
Brioude [F] 32 E2
Brioux–sur–Boutonne [F] 24 C2
Briouze [F] 10 D3
Brissac–Quincé [F] 16 F3
Brive–la–Gaillarde [F] 32 B2
Broglie [F] 10 E3
Brommat [F] 32 D3
Bron [F] 34 C1
Broons [F] 8 E4
Brossac [F] 24 C4
Brou [F] 18 D2
Brouage [F] 24 B3
Brouis, Col de– [F] 42 D2
Brouvelieures [F] 22 C3
Brouwershaven [NL] 4 E2
Bruère–Allichamps [F] 26 C2
Brugge [B] 4 D3
Brûlon [F] 18 A2
Brumath [F] 22 E2
Brummen [NL] 6 D2
Brunehamel [F] 12 F2
Bruniquel [F] 32 B4
Brunssum [NL] 6 C4
Brussel / Bruxelles [B] 4 F4
Bruxelles / Brussel [B] 4 F4
Bruyères [F] 22 C3
Bubry [F] 8 C4
Buchy [F] 12 A2
Bucquoy [F] 12 D1

Bugeat [F] 26 A4
Buis–les–Baronnies [F] 40 E1
Buitenpost [NL] 2 D2
Bulgnéville [F] 20 F3
Bunleix [F] 26 B4
Buoux, Fort de– [F] 40 E2
Burgh–Haamstede [NL] 4 E2
Burie [F] 24 C3
Buron, Château de– [F] 32 E1
Bussang [F] 22 C4
Bussang, Col de– [F] 22 D4
Bussum [NL] 2 B4
Bütgenbach [B] 14 C2
Buxy [F] 26 F3
Buzançais [F] 26 A1
Buzancy [F] 14 A3

C

Cabourg [F] 10 D2
Cabrerets [F] 32 B3
Cadenet [F] 40 E2
Cadillac [F] 30 D2
Caen [F] 10 D2
Cagnes–sur–Mer [F] 42 C3
Cahors [F] 32 B3
Cajarc [F] 32 B3
Calacuccia [F] 44 B2
Calais [F] 4 B3
Calenzana [F] 44 B2
Calignac [F] 30 E3
Callac [F] 8 C3
Calvi [F] 44 B2
Camarès [F] 38 E1
Camaret–sur–Mer [F] 8 A3
Cambo–les–Bains [F] 36 C2
Cambrai [F] 12 D1
Cambremer [F] 10 E3
Campan [F] 36 E3
Cancale [F] 8 F3
Cancon [F] 30 E3
Candé [F] 16 E2
Canet [F] 40 B2
Canet–Plage [F] 38 E4
Cannes [F] 42 C3
Cany–Barville [F] 10 F2
Capbreton [F] 30 A4
Cap–d'Ail [F] 42 D3
Capdenac–Gare [F] 32 C3
Capendu [F] 38 D3
Capens [F] 38 B2
Capestang [F] 38 E2
Cap Ferret [F] 30 B2
Capo Cavallo [F] 44 A2
Captieux [F] 30 D3
Caraman [F] 38 C2
Carantec [F] 8 C2
Carbon–Blanc [F] 30 C1
Carbonne [F] 38 B2
Carcans [F] 30 C1
Carcans–Plage [F] 24 A4
Carcassonne [F] 38 D2
Carcès [F] 40 F3
Carennac [F] 32 B2
Carentan [F] 10 C2
Cargèse [F] 44 A2
Carhaix–Plouguer [F] 8 C3
Carignan [F] 14 B3
Carling [F] 22 D1
Carmaux [F] 32 C4
Caro [F] 16 C1
Carpentras [F] 40 D1
Carquefou [F] 16 D3
Carqueiranne [F] 40 F4

Carro [F] 40 D3
Carrouges [F] 10 D4
Carry–le–Rouet [F] 40 D3
Carteret [F] 10 B2
Casamozza [F] 44 C2
Cassagnes–Bégonhès [F] 32 C4
Cassel [F] 4 C4
Cassis [F] 40 E3
Castanet–Tolosan [F] 38 C2
Casteau [B] 12 F1
Castelbouc [F] 32 E4
Casteljaloux [F] 30 D3
Castellane [F] 42 B2
Castelmoron [F] 30 E3
Castelnau [F] 32 B2
Castelnaudary [F] 38 D2
Castelnau–de–Médoc [F] 30 C1
Castelnau–de–Montmiral [F] 32 B4
Castelnau D'Estretefonds [F] 38 C1
Castelnau–Magnoac [F] 36 F3
Castelnau–Montratier [F] 30 F3
Castelsarrasin [F] 30 F4
Castets [F] 30 B3
Castillon–la–Bataille [F] 30 D2
Castillonnès [F] 30 E2
Castres [F] 38 D2
Castricum [NL] 2 B3
Castries [F] 40 B2
Cateraggio [F] 44 C3
Catus [F] 32 A3
Caudebec [F] 10 F2
Caudeval [F] 38 C3
Caudry [F] 12 E2
Caumont [F] 10 C2
Caumont [F] 38 B2
Caunes–Minervois [F] 38 D2
Cauro [F] 44 B3
Caussade [F] 32 B4
Cauterets [F] 36 D3
Cauville [F] 10 E2
Cavaillon [F] 40 D2
Cavalaire–sur–Mer [F] 42 B4
Cavalière [F] 42 B4
Caylus [F] 32 B3
Cayres [F] 32 C2
Cazals [F] 30 F3
Cazaubon [F] 30 D4
Cazeneuve, Château de– [F] 30 D3
Cazères [F] 38 B2
Ceillac [F] 34 E4
Celles [B] 4 D4
Celles–sur–Belle [F] 24 D2
Centuri [F] 44 C1
Céret [F] 38 D4
Cerfontaine [B] 12 F2
Cérilly [F] 26 C2
Cerisiers [F] 20 B2
Cerizay [F] 16 E4
Cernay [F] 22 D4
Cerniébaud [F] 28 B4
Cervione [F] 44 C2
Cessenon–sur–Orb [F] 38 E2
Ceyzériat [F] 28 B4
Chaalis, Abbaye de– [F] 12 C3
Chabanais [F] 24 E3
Chabeuil [F] 34 B3
Chablis [F] 20 C3
Chabreloche [F] 26 D4
Chabris [F] 18 D4
Chagny [F] 28 A2
Chailland [F] 16 F1
Chaillé–les–Marais [F] 24 B2

Chailley–Turny [F] 20 B3
Chailluz, Fort de– [F] 28 C2
Chalabre [F] 38 C3
Chalais [F] 24 C4
Chalamont [F] 28 A4
Chalampé [F] 22 D4
Challans [F] 16 D3
Challes–les–Eaux [F] 34 D2
Chalonnes [F] 16 E3
Chalonnes–sur–Loire [F] 16 E3
Châlons–en–Champagne [F] 20 D1
Chalon–sur–Saône [F] 28 A2
Châlus [F] 24 E4
Chalusset, Château de– [F] 24 F4
Chambéret [F] 24 F4
Chambéry [F] 34 D2
Chambley–Bussières [F] 20 F1
Chambon–sur–Lac [F] 32 D1
Chambon–sur–Voueize [F] 26 B3
Chambord [F] 18 D3
Chambord, Parc de– [F] 18 D3
Chamelet [F] 26 E4
Chamonix–Mont–Blanc [F] 34 F1
Champagnac–le–Vieux [F] 32 E2
Champagne–Mouton [F] 24 D3
Champagnole [F] 28 C3
Champaubert [F] 20 C1
Champdeniers [F] 24 C2
Champeix [F] 32 E1
Champ du Feu [F] 22 D3
Champeix [F] 32 E1
Champier [F] 34 C2
Champigné [F] 16 F2
Champigny–sur–Veude [F] 18 B4
Champillon [F] 12 E4
Champlitte [F] 20 E4
Champlon [B] 14 B2
Champrond–en–Gâtine [F] 18 D1
Champtoceaux [F] 16 E3
Chamrousse [F] 34 D3
Chanas [F] 34 B2
Chantelle [F] 26 D3
Chantemerle [F] 34 E3
Chantilly [F] 12 C3
Chantonnay [F] 16 E4
Chaource [F] 20 C3
Chapelle–Royale [F] 18 D2
Charavines [F] 34 C2
Charbonnières–les–Bains [F] 34 B1
Charenton–du–Cher [F] 26 C2
Charité, Abbaye de la– [F] 28 C1
Charleville–Mézières [F] 14 A3
Charlieu [F] 26 E4
Charly [F] 12 D4
Charmes [F] 22 C3
Charny [F] 20 A3
Charolles [F] 26 E3
Chârost [F] 26 B1
Charpentry [F] 14 A4
Charroux [F] 24 D3
Chartres [F] 18 D1
Chasseneuil–s.–Bonnieure [F] 24 D3
Chasse sur Rhone [F] 34 B2

Chassigny [F] 20 E4
Château–Arnoux [F] 40 F2
Châteaubourg [F] 16 E1
Châteaubriant [F] 16 E2
Château–Chinon [F] 26 E2
Château–du–Loir [F] 18 B2
Châteaudun [F] 18 D2
Châteaugiron [F] 16 E1
Château–Gontier [F] 16 F2
Château–la–Vallière [F] 18 B3
Château–L'Évêque [F] 30 E1
Châteaulin [F] 8 B3
Châteaumeillant [F] 26 B2
Châteauneuf [F] 24 C3
Châteauneuf–de–Randon [F] 32 E3
Châteauneuf–du–Faou [F] 8 C3
Châteauneuf–du–Pape [F] 40 D1
Châteauneuf–en–Thymerais [F] 10 F4
Chateauneuf–sur–Cher [F] 26 B2
Châteauneuf–sur–Sarthe [F] 16 F2
Châteauponsac [F] 24 F3
Château–Porcien [F] 12 F3
Château–Queyras [F] 34 E4
Château–Regnault [F] 14 A2
Châteaurenard [F] 20 A3
Château–Renault [F] 18 C3
Châteauroux [F] 26 A2
Château–Salins [F] 22 C2
Château–Thierry [F] 12 D4
Châteauvillain [F] 20 D3
Châtel [F] 28 D4
Châtelaillon–Plage [F] 24 B2
Châtelet [B] 14 A1
Châtelguyon [F] 26 C4
Châtellerault [F] 24 E1
Châtel–Montagne [F] 26 D4
Châtelus–Malvaleix [F] 26 B3
Châtenois [F] 20 F3
Châtillon–Coligny [F] 18 F3
Châtillon–en–Bazois [F] 26 E2
Châtillon–en–Diois [F] 34 C4
Châtillon–sur–Chalaronne [F] 28 A4
Châtillon–sur–Indre [F] 18 C4
Châtillon–sur–Loire [F] 18 F3
Châtillon–sur–Marne [F] 12 E4
Châtillon–sur–Seine [F] 20 D3
Châtre, Église de– [F] 24 C3
Chaudes–Aigues [F] 32 D3
Chauffailles [F] 26 E3
Chaufour–lès–Bonnières [F] 12 A3
Chaumergy [F] 28 B2
Chaumont [F] 18 C3
Chaumont [F] 20 E3
Chaumont–sur–Aire [F] 20 E1
Chaumont–sur–Loire [F] 18 C3
Chaunay [F] 24 D2
Chauny [F] 12 D3
Chaussin [F] 28 B2
Chauvigny [F] 24 E2
Chaux–Neuve [F] 28 C3
Chazelles [F] 34 B1
Chazelles–sur–Lyon [F] 34 B1
Chef–Boutonne [F] 24 D2
Chemillé [F] 16 E3
Chemin [F] 28 B2

Chêne-Pignier [F] 24 E3
Chénérailles [F] 26 B3
Chenonceaux [F] 18 C3
Cherbourg [F] 10 B1
Chéroy [F] 20 A2
Cherveix-Cubas [F] 32 A1
Chevagnes [F] 26 D2
Chevanceaux [F] 24 C4
Chevilly, Château de- [F] 18 E2
Chevreuse [F] 12 B4
Chézal-Benoît [F] 26 B2
Chimay [B] 12 F2
Chinon [F] 18 B3
Chisa [F] 44 B3
Cholet [F] 16 E3
Chorges [F] 34 D4
Chouvigny, Gorges de- [F] 26 C3
Choye [F] 28 C1
Ciboure [F] 36 B2
Cierp-Gaud [F] 36 F3
Ciney [B] 14 B2
Cintegabelle [F] 38 C2
Cirey [F] 22 D2
Ciron [F] 24 F2
Cîteaux, Abbaye de- [F] 28 B2
Civray [F] 24 D2
Civrieux-d'Azergues [F] 34 B1
Clairvaux-les-Lacs [F] 28 C3
Clamecy [F] 20 B4
Clamouse, Grotte de- [F] 40 B2
Clécy [F] 10 D3
Clefmont [F] 20 E3
Clefs [F] 18 B2
Clelles [F] 34 C3
Cléon-d'Andran [F] 34 B4
Clères [F] 12 A2
Clermont [F] 12 C3
Clermont-de-Beauregarde [F] 30 E2
Clermont-en-Argonne [F] 14 A4
Clermont-Ferrand [F] 26 C4
Clermont-l'Hérault [F] 38 F2
Clerval [F] 28 D2
Clervaux [L] 14 C2
Cléry [F] 18 D3
Clisson [F] 16 E3
Cloyes-sur-le-Loir [F] 18 D2
Cluny [F] 26 F3
Cluses [F] 34 E1
Coevorden [NL] 2 E3
Coflans [F] 34 E2
Cognac [F] 24 C3
Cogolin [F] 42 B4
Cohiniac [F] 8 D3
Colembert [F] 4 B4
Coligny [F] 28 B3
Collinée [F] 8 D4
Collioure [F] 38 E4
Collonges [F] 28 C4
Collonges-la-Rouge [F] 32 B2
Colmar [F] 22 D3
Colmars [F] 42 B2
Cologne [F] 38 B1
Colombey-les-Belles [F] 20 F2
Colombey-les-Deux-Églises [F] 20 D3
Colomiers [F] 38 C1
Combeaufontaine [F] 20 F4
Combourg [F] 8 F4
Combronde [F] 26 C4
Commentry [F] 26 C3
Commequiers [F] 16 D4

Commercy [F] 20 F2
Compiègne [F] 12 C3
Comps-sur-Artuby [F] 42 B3
Concarneau [F] 8 B4
Conches [F] 10 E3
Condat [F] 32 D2
Condé-en-Brie [F] 12 D4
Condé-sur-Noireau [F] 10 D3
Condom [F] 30 D4
Condrieu [F] 34 B2
Conflans en Jarnisy [F] 14 B4
Confolens [F] 24 E3
Conlie [F] 18 B1
Connerré [F] 18 C2
Conques [F] 32 C3
Contay [F] 12 C2
Contres [F] 18 D3
Contrexéville [F] 20 F3
Conty [F] 12 C2
Coray [F] 8 B4
Corbeil-Essonnes [F] 18 F1
Corbeny [F] 12 E3
Corbie [F] 12 C2
Corbigny [F] 26 E1
Corcieux [F] 22 D3
Corconne [F] 40 B2
Cordes [F] 32 B4
Corlay [F] 8 D3
Cormainville [F] 18 D2
Cormeilles [F] 10 E3
Cormery [F] 18 C3
Cornimont [F] 22 C3
Corps [F] 34 D3
Corre [F] 20 F3
Corte [F] 44 B2
Cosne [F] 18 F4
Cosne d'Allier [F] 26 C3
Cossé-le-Vivien [F] 16 F2
Cotignac [F] 40 F3
Couches [F] 26 F2
Coucy [F] 12 E4
Coudray-Montbault, Château de- [F] 16 F3
Couflenz [F] 38 B3
Cougnac, Grottes de- [F] 32 B2
Couhé [F] 24 D2
Couilly [F] 12 C4
Couiza [F] 38 D3
Coulanges-la-Vineuse [F] 20 B3
Coulommiers [F] 20 B1
Coulon [F] 24 C2
Coulonges [F] 24 C1
Couptrain [F] 10 D4
Courboyer, Manoir de- [F] 18 C1
Courchevel [F] 34 E2
Cour-Cheverny [F] 18 D3
Courçon [F] 24 C2
Cour-et-Buis [F] 34 C2
Courgains [F] 18 B1
Courpière [F] 32 E1
Coursan [F] 38 E3
Courseulles-sur-Mer [F] 10 D2
Cours-la-Ville [F] 26 E4
Courson-les-Carrières [F] 20 B3
Courtacon [F] 20 B1
Courtanvaux, Château de- [F] 18 C2
Courteilles [F] 10 E3
Courtenay [F] 20 A2
Courtomer [F] 10 E4
Courtrail (Kortrijk) [B] 4 D4
Courville [F] 18 D1
Coutances [F] 10 B2

Couterne [F] 10 D4
Coutevroult [F] 12 C4
Coutras [F] 30 D1
Couvin [B] 12 F2
Cox [F] 38 B1
Cozes [F] 24 B3
Cozzano [F] 44 B3
Craon [F] 16 E2
Craponne-sur-Arzon [F] 32 F2
Crêches-sur-Saône [F] 26 F4
Crécy [F] 12 C4
Crécy-en-Ponthieu [F] 12 B1
Crécy-sur-Serre [F] 12 E3
Creil [F] 12 C3
Crémieu [F] 34 C1
Créon [F] 30 D2
Crépy-en-Valois [F] 12 C3
Crespin [F] 12 E1
Cressensac [F] 32 B2
Crest [F] 34 B3
Creutzwald [F] 14 D4
Crevecoeur [F] 12 B2
Crocq [F] 26 B4
Croix Haute, Col de la- [F] 34 C4
Cro-Magnon [F] 30 F2
Crozant [F] 26 A2
Crozon [F] 8 B3
Cruas [F] 34 B3
Cruseilles [F] 34 E1
Cruzy [F] 38 E2
Cuers [F] 40 F3
Cuhom [F] 4 C4
Cuijk [NL] 6 C2
Cuiseaux [F] 28 B3
Cuisery [F] 28 A3
Culan [F] 26 B2
Culemborg [NL] 6 B2
Culoz [F] 34 D1
Cunault [F] 18 A3
Curel [F] 40 E1
Cusset [F] 26 D3
Cuvilly [F] 12 C3

D

Dabo [F] 22 D2
Dabo, Roch. de- [F] 22 D2
Daluis, Gorges de- [F] 42 C2
Dammartin-en-Goële [F] 12 C4
Damparis [F] 28 B2
Dampierre [F] 12 B4
Dampierre [F] 28 C2
Dampierre-sur-Boutonne [F] 24 C2
Dampierre-sur-Salon [F] 20 E4
Damville [F] 10 F4
Damvillers [F] 14 B4
Dangé-St-Romain [F] 18 B4
Dannemarie [F] 28 E1
Daon [F] 16 F2
Daoulas [F] 8 B3
Dargilan, Grotte de- [F] 32 E4
Darney [F] 20 F3
Dax [F] 30 B4
Deauville [F] 10 E2
Decazeville [F] 32 C3
Decines [F] 34 C1
Decize [F] 26 D2
De Cocksdorp [NL] 2 B2
Dedemsvaart [NL] 2 D3

Defile de L'Ecluse [F] 28 C4
De Haan [B] 4 D3
Deinze [B] 4 E4
De Koog [NL] 2 B2
De Kooy [NL] 2 B2
Delden [NL] 2 E4
Delft [NL] 2 A4
Delfzijl [NL] 2 E2
Delle [F] 28 E1
Delme [F] 22 C1
Delouze-Rosières [F] 20 E2
Demigny [F] 28 A2
Demoiselles, Grotte des- [F] 40 B1
Denain [F] 12 E1
Den Burg [NL] 2 B2
Dendermonde [B] 4 E4
Denekamp [NL] 2 E4
Den Haag [NL] 2 A4
Den Helder [NL] 2 B2
Den Oever [NL] 2 C2
De Panne [B] 4 C3
Derval [F] 16 D2
Descartes [F] 18 B4
Desvres [F] 4 B4
Deurne [NL] 6 C3
Deventer [NL] 2 D4
Die [F] 34 C3
Diekirch [L] 14 C3
Dienne [F] 32 D2
Dieppe [F] 12 A1
Dieren [NL] 6 D2
Diest [B] 6 B4
Dieue-sur-Meuse [F] 20 E1
Dieulefit [F] 34 B4
Dieulouard [F] 22 C2
Dieuze [F] 22 C2
Diever [NL] 2 D3
Differdange [L] 14 C3
Dignac [F] 24 D4
Digne-les-Bains [F] 42 B2
Digny [F] 18 D1
Digoin [F] 26 E3
Dijon [F] 28 B1
Diksmuide [B] 4 D3
Dinan [F] 8 E3
Dinant [B] 14 A2
Dinard [F] 8 E3
Dinozé [F] 22 C3
Disneyland Paris [F] 12 C4
Dives-sur-Mer [F] 10 D2
Divonne-les-Bains [F] 28 C4
Doesburg [NL] 6 D2
Doetinchem [NL] 6 D2
Dokkum [NL] 2 D2
Dol-de-Bretagne [F] 8 F3
Dole [F] 28 B2
Dombasle [F] 22 C2
Dombrot-le-Sec [F] 20 F3
Domburg [NL] 4 E2
Domèvre-en-Haye [F] 20 F2
Domfront [F] 10 C4
Domme [F] 30 F2
Dompaire [F] 22 C3
Dompierre [F] 26 D3
Dompierre-du-Chemin [F] 10 B4
Dompierre-sur-Besbre [F] 26 D3
Dompierre-sur-Mer [F] 24 B2
Domrémy-la-Pucelle [F] 20 F2
Dontilly [F] 20 B2
Donzenac [F] 32 B1
Donzère [F] 34 B4
Donzy [F] 20 A4
Doorn [NL] 6 C2
Dordives [F] 18 F2
Dordrecht [NL] 6 B2
Dormans [F] 12 E4

Dornas [F] 34 A3
Dornes [F] 26 D2
Dortan [F] 28 B4
Douai [F] 12 D1
Douamont, Fort du- [F] 14 B4
Douarnenez [F] 8 B3
Douchy [F] 20 A3
Doucier [F] 28 C3
Doudeville [F] 10 F2
Doué-la-Fontaine [F] 16 F3
Doulaincourt [F] 20 E2
Doulevant-le-Château [F] 20 D2
Doullens [F] 12 C1
Dourdan [F] 18 E1
Dourgne [F] 38 D2
Douvaine [F] 28 C4
Douzy [F] 14 A3
Dozulé [F] 10 E2
Drachten [NL] 2 D2
Dragon, Caverne du- [F] 12 E3
Draguignan [F] 42 B3
Dreux [F] 12 A4
Driebergen [NL] 6 C2
Drionville [F] 4 B4
Dronten [NL] 2 C3
Drusenheim [F] 22 E2
Druten [NL] 6 C2
Ducey [F] 10 B3
Duclair [F] 10 F2
Dudelange [L] 14 C4
Duingt [F] 34 E1
Dun [F] 14 A4
Dunkerque [F] 4 C3
Dunkerque Ouest [F] 4 C3
Dun-le-Palestel [F] 26 A3
Dun-sur-Auron [F] 26 C2
Duras [F] 30 D2
Durban-Corbières [F] 38 E3
Durbuy [B] 14 B2
Durtal [F] 18 A2
Dwingeloo [NL] 2 D3

E

Eaux-Bonnes [F] 36 D3
Eaux-Chaudes [F] 36 D3
Eauze [F] 30 D4
Ebreuil [F] 26 C3
Echallon [F] 28 B4
Échourgnac [F] 30 E1
Echternach [L] 14 C3
Ecole Valentine [F] 28 C2
Ecommoy [F] 18 B2
Ecouis [F] 12 A3
Ecueillé [F] 18 C4
Ecury [F] 20 D1
Edam [NL] 2 B3
Ede [NL] 6 C2
Eeklo [B] 4 E3
Eghezée [B] 14 B1
Egletons [F] 32 C1
Egmond aan Zee [NL] 2 B3
Eguzon [F] 26 A2
Ehnen [L] 14 C3
Eibergen [NL] 6 D2
Eindhoven [NL] 6 C3
Elbeuf [F] 10 F3
Elburg [NL] 2 C4
Elne [F] 38 E4
Elst [NL] 6 C2
Elven, Tour d'- [F] 16 C1
Emberménil [F] 22 C2
Embrun [F] 34 E4

Emmeloord [NL] 2 C3
Emmen [NL] 2 E3
Englefontaine [F] 12 E1
Enkhuizen [NL] 2 C3
Ennezat [F] 26 D4
Enschede [NL] 2 E4
Ensisheim [F] 22 D4
Entraigues [F] 18 D4
Entraygues-sur-Truyère [F] 32 C3
Entrevaux [F] 42 C2
Epannes [F] 24 C2
Epe [NL] 2 D4
Épernay [F] 12 E4
Épernon [F] 18 E1
Épinal [F] 22 C3
Epiry [F] 26 E1
Epône [F] 12 B4
Erbalunga [F] 44 C1
Ermelo [F] 2 C4
Ermenonville [F] 12 C3
Ermitage, Grotte de l'– [F] 28 B2
Ernée [F] 10 C4
Erquy [F] 8 E3
Erstein [F] 22 E3
Ervy-le-Châtel [F] 20 C3
Esch-sur-Alzette [L] 14 C3
Esch-sur-Sûre [L] 14 C3
Escos [F] 36 C2
Esnouveaux [F] 20 E3
Espalion [F] 32 D3
Espelette [F] 36 B2
Espezel [F] 38 C3
Esplantas [F] 32 E3
Essoyes [F] 20 D3
Estagel [F] 38 E3
Estaing [F] 32 D3
Estaires [F] 4 C4
Esternay [F] 20 C1
Estissac [F] 20 C2
Estrées-St-Denis [F] 12 C3
Étables-sur-Mer [F] 8 D3
Étain [F] 14 B4
Étalle [B] 14 B3
Étampes [F] 18 E1
Étang-sur-Arroux [F] 26 E2
Étaples [F] 4 B4
Étoges [F] 20 C1
Étréaupont [F] 12 E2
Étrepagny [F] 12 B3
Étretat [F] 10 E2
Ettelbruck [L] 14 C3
Eu [F] 12 B1
Eugénie-les-Bains [F] 30 C4
Eupen [B] 14 C1
Europoort [NL] 2 A4
Evaux-les-Bains [F] 26 B3
Evian-les-Bains [F] 28 D4
Evisa [F] 44 B2
Evran [F] 8 E4
Evreux [F] 10 F3
Evron [F] 18 A1
Evry [F] 18 F1
Excideuil [F] 30 F1
Exmes [F] 10 E4
Eyguières [F] 40 D2
Eygurande [F] 26 B4
Eylie [F] 36 F4
Eymet [F] 30 E2
Eymoutiers [F] 26 A4

F

Facture [F] 30 C2
Fageole, Col de la– [F] 32 E2
Falaise [F] 10 D3
Falkenstein, Château de– [F] 22 E1
Fanjeaux [F] 38 D2
Farcheville, Château de– [F] 18 F1
Farébersviller [F] 22 D1
Faucille, Col de la– [F] 28 C4
Faucogney-et-la-Mer [F] 22 C4
Faulquemont [F] 22 C1
Fauville [F] 10 F2
Faverges [F] 34 E2
Faverney [F] 20 F4
Favone [F] 44 C3
Fayence [F] 42 B3
Fayet [F] 38 E1
Fayl-Billot [F] 20 E4
Fay-sur-Lignon [F] 34 A3
Fécamp [F] 10 E2
Felletin [F] 26 B4
Fénétrange [F] 22 D2
Feneu [F] 16 F2
Fer a Cheval, Cirque du– [F] 28 C2
Fère, Château de– [F] 12 D4
Fère-Champenoise [F] 20 C1
Fère-en-Tardenois [F] 12 D4
Ferrette [F] 28 E1
Ferrières [F] 18 F2
Ferrières-sur-Sichon [F] 26 D4
Feu, Roche du– [F] 8 B3
Feurs [F] 34 B1
Fier, Gorges du– [F] 34 D1
Figari [F] 44 B4
Figeac [F] 32 C3
Filitosa [F] 44 B3
Firminy [F] 34 A2
Fismes [F] 12 E3
Flaine [F] 34 F1
Flaran [F] 30 D4
Flaugeac [F] 30 E2
Flavigny-sur-Moselle [F] 22 C2
Fléchin [F] 4 C4
Fleckenstein, Château de– [F] 22 E1
Flers [F] 10 D3
Fleurance [F] 30 E4
Fleuré [F] 24 E2
Fleurus [B] 14 A1
Fleury [F] 12 A3
Flins [F] 12 B4
Flize [F] 14 A3
Flogny-la-Chapelle [F] 20 C3
Florac [F] 32 E4
Florange [F] 14 C4
Florennes [B] 14 A2
Florenville [B] 14 B3
Flumet [F] 34 E1
Foix [F] 38 C3
Folelli [F] 44 C2
Fondamente [F] 38 F1
Fontainebleau [F] 18 F2
Fontaine-de-Vaucluse [F] 40 D2
Fontaine-Française [F] 20 E4
Fontaine Guérard, Abbaye de– [F] 12 A3
Fontaine Henry, Château de– [F] 10 D2
Fontaine-le-Dun [F] 10 F2
Fontaine-sur-Coole [F] 20 D1
Fontenay, Abbaye de– [F] 20 C4
Fontenay-le-Comte [F] 24 C1
Fontenay-Trésigny [F] 20 B1
Fontevraud-l'Abbaye [F] 18 B3
Fontfroide, Abbaye de– [F] 38 E3
Fontgombault [F] 24 F2
Font-Romeu [F] 38 C4
Fontvieille [F] 40 D2
Forbach [F] 22 D1
Forcalquier [F] 40 F2
Forges-les-Eaux [F] 12 B2
Formerie [F] 12 B2
Formiguères [F] 38 C4
Fos [F] 36 F4
Fosses [B] 14 A1
Fos-sur-Mer [F] 40 D3
Foucarmont [F] 12 B2
Fouesnant [F] 8 B4
Fougères [F] 10 B4
Fougerolles [F] 22 C4
Foulain [F] 20 E3
Fouras [F] 24 B2
Fourcès [F] 30 D4
Fourmies [F] 12 E2
Fourneaux [F] 26 B3
Fournels [F] 32 D3
Fourquet [F] 30 E3
Fours [F] 26 E2
Fraize [F] 22 D3
Framzelle [F] 4 B3
Francardo [F] 44 B2
Franeker [NL] 2 C2
Frangy [F] 34 D1
Frayssinet [F] 32 B3
Fréjus [F] 42 B3
Fresnay-sur-Sarthe [F] 18 B1
Fresnes [F] 12 D1
Fresnes [F] 20 F3
Fresnes-en-Woëvre [F] 20 F1
Fréteval [F] 18 D2
Fretigney-et-Velloreille [F] 28 C1
Frévent [F] 12 C1
Freyming Merlebach [F] 22 D1
Froissy [F] 12 C2
Fromental [F] 10 D3
Fronsac [F] 36 F3
Frontignan [F] 40 B2
Fronton [F] 32 A4
Fumay [F] 14 A2
Fumel [F] 30 F3
Furnes (Veurne) [B] 4 C3

G

Gaasbeek [B] 4 F4
Gabarret [F] 30 D3
Gacé [F] 10 E3
Gaël [F] 8 E4
Gaillac [F] 38 D1
Gaillon [F] 12 A3
Galan [F] 36 E3
Galéria [F] 44 A2
Gallargues [F] 40 C2
Gamaches-en-Vexin [F] 12 B1
Gan [F] 36 D2
Ganagobie, Prieuré– [F] 40 F2
Gand (Gent) [B] 4 E4
Ganges [F] 40 B1
Gannat [F] 26 C3
Gap [F] 34 D4
Gard, Pont du– [F] 40 C2
Gardanne [F] 40 E3
Garein [F] 30 C3
Gargas, Grotte de– [F] 36 F3
Gargilesse-Dampierre [F] 26 A2
Gaubert [F] 18 D2
Gauville [F] 10 E3
Gavarnie [F] 36 E4
Gavarnie, Cirque de– [F] 36 E4
Gavray [F] 10 B3
Gedinne [B] 14 A2
Geel [B] 6 B4
Geertruidenberg [NL] 6 B2
Geldrop [NL] 6 C3
Geleen [NL] 6 C4
Gembloux [B] 14 A1
Gémenos [F] 40 E3
Gemert [NL] 6 C3
Gémozac [F] 24 B3
Genappe [B] 14 A1
Gençay [F] 24 E2
Génelard [F] 26 E3
Genillé [F] 18 C4
Genk [B] 6 B4
Genlis [F] 28 B2
Gennep [NL] 6 C3
Gennes [F] 18 A3
Génolhac [F] 32 F4
Gent (Gand) [B] 4 E4
Gentioux [F] 26 A4
Geraardsbergen [B] 4 E4
Gérardmer [F] 22 D3
Gerbéviller [F] 22 C2
Germay [F] 20 E2
Germigny-Des-Pres [F] 18 E3
Gevrey-Chambertin [F] 28 B2
Gex [F] 28 C4
Ghisonaccia [F] 44 C3
Ghisoni [F] 44 B3
Giat [F] 26 B4
Gien [F] 40 F4
Giens [F] 40 F4
Gieten [NL] 2 E3
Giethoorn [NL] 2 D3
Gignac [F] 40 B2
Gimat [F] 30 E4
Gimel-les-Cascades [F] 32 C1
Gimont [F] 38 B1
Girolata [F] 44 A2
Giromagny [F] 22 C4
Gisors [F] 12 B3
Gistel [B] 4 D3
Givet [F] 14 A2
Givors [F] 34 B2
Givry [B] 12 F1
Givry [F] 26 F2
Givry-en-Argonne [F] 20 E1
Gizeux [F] 18 B3
Glénic [F] 26 B3
Gneux [F] 12 E4
Goderville [F] 10 E2
Goes [NL] 4 E3
Goirle [NL] 6 B3
Golfe-Juan [F] 42 C3
Golfo di Sogno [F] 44 B4
Goncelin [F] 34 D2
Gondrecourt [F] 20 E2
Gondrin [F] 30 D4
Gooik [B] 4 E4
Goor [NL] 2 D4
Gordes [F] 40 E2
Gorinchem [NL] 6 B2
Gorredijk [NL] 2 D2
Gorron [F] 10 C4
Gouarec [F] 8 C3
Gouda [NL] 6 B2
Goules, Col des– [F] 26 C4
Gourdon [F] 32 B2
Gourin [F] 8 C3
Gournay-en-Bray [F] 12 B2
Gourville [F] 24 D3
Gouzon [F] 26 B3
Graçay [F] 18 D4
Gradignan [F] 30 C2
Grainetière, Abbaye de la– [F] 16 E4
Gramat [F] 32 B2
Grancey [F] 20 D4
Grandcamp-Maisy [F] 10 C2
Grand-Champ [F] 16 C1
Grand Chartreuse, Couvent de la– [F] 34 D2
Grande-Fougeray [F] 16 D2
Grandpré [F] 14 A4
Grandrieu [F] 32 E3
Grand Roc [F] 30 F2
Grandvilliers [F] 12 B2
Grange-Bleneau, Château de la– [F] 20 B1
Grange-le-Bocage [F] 20 B2
Granges-sur-Vologne [F] 22 D3
Granville [F] 10 B3
Grasse [F] 42 C3
Graulhet [F] 38 D1
Grave [NL] 6 C2
Gravelines [F] 4 C3
Gray [F] 28 C1
Grenade [F] 30 C4
Grenade [F] 38 C1
Grenoble [F] 34 D3
Gréolierès [F] 42 C2
Gréoux-les-Bains [F] 40 F2
Greux [F] 20 F2
Grevenmacher [L] 14 C3
Grez-en-Bouère [F] 16 F2
Grignan [F] 34 B4
Grignols [F] 30 D3
Grimaud [F] 42 B3
Grisolles [F] 32 A4
Groenlo [NL] 6 D2
Groix [F] 16 B1
Groningen [NL] 2 E2
Grostenquin [F] 22 D1
Grouw [NL] 2 D2
Gruissan [F] 38 E3
Guagno [F] 44 B2
Guebwiller [F] 22 D4
Guémené-Penfao [F] 16 D2
Guémené-sur-Scorff [F] 8 C4
Guenange [F] 14 C4
Guer [F] 16 D1
Guérande [F] 16 C2
Guéret [F] 26 A3
Guérigny [F] 26 D1
Guethary [F] 30 A4
Gueugnon [F] 26 E3
Guichen [F] 16 D1
Guignes [F] 20 A1
Guillaumes [F] 42 C2
Guillestre [F] 34 E4
Guilvinec [F] 8 B4
Guimiliau [F] 8 B3
Guînes [F] 4 B3
Guingamp [F] 8 D3
Guipry [F] 16 D1
Guise [F] 12 E2
Guissény [F] 8 B2
Guîtres [F] 30 D1
Gujan-Mestras [F] 30 B2
Gurgazu [F] 44 B4
Guzet-Neige [F] 38 B3
Gy [F] 28 C1

H

Haaksbergen [NL] 6 E2
Haarlem [NL] 2 B3
Habay [B] 14 B3
Hagetmau [F] 30 C4
Hagondange [F] 14 C4
Haguenau [F] 22 E2
Hallignicourt [F] 20 D2
Halluin [F] 4 D4
Halsteren [NL] 4 F3
Ham [F] 12 D2
Hambye, Abbaye de- [F] 10 C3
Hamoir [B] 14 B1
Hannuit (Hannut) [B] 14 B1
Hannut (Hannuit) [B] 14 B1
Han-sur-Lesse [B] 14 B2
Han-sur-Nied [F] 22 C1
Haras du Pin [F] 10 E4
Hardelot-Plage [F] 4 B4
Hardenberg [NL] 2 E3
Harderwijk [NL] 2 C4
Haren [NL] 2 E2
Harfleur [F] 10 E2
Harlingen [NL] 2 C2
Haroué [F] 22 C2
Hasparren [F] 36 C2
Hasselt [B] 6 B4
Hasselt [NL] 2 D3
Hastiere-Lavaux [B] 14 A2
Hattem [NL] 2 D3
Hattonchâtel [F] 20 F1
Haule [NL] 2 D2
Haut-Asco [F] 44 B2
Haut-Barr, Château du- [F] 22 D2
Hautecombe, Abbaye de- [F] 34 D1
Hautefort, Château de- [F] 32 B1
Hauteville-Lompnes [F] 34 D1
Hauteville Plage [F] 10 B2
Haut Koenigsbourg [F] 22 D3
Hautmont [F] 12 E1
Havelange [B] 14 B1
Hayange [F] 14 C4
Hazebrouck [F] 4 C4
Hechtel [B] 6 B4
Hédé [F] 8 F4
Heemstede [NL] 2 B3
Heerde [NL] 2 D3
Heerenveen [NL] 2 D2
Heeze [NL] 6 B3
Heino [NL] 2 D4
Hellendoorn [NL] 2 D4
Hellevoetsluis [NL] 4 F2
Helmond [NL] 6 C3
Hèming [F] 22 D2
Hendaye [F] 36 B2
Hengelo [NL] 2 E3
Hénin Beaumont [F] 12 D1
Hennebont [F] 16 B1
Henrichemont [F] 18 E4
Hérault, Gorges de l'- [F] 40 B2
Herbault [F] 18 C3
Herbesthal [B] 14 C1
Herbeumont [B] 14 B3
Herbignac [F] 16 C2
Herentals [B] 6 B3
Héricourt [F] 28 D1
Hérisson [F] 26 C2
Herment [F] 26 B4
Herselt [B] 6 B4
Het Loo [NL] 2 D4
Hettange-Grande [F] 14 C4

Heyrieux [F] 34 C2
Hiersac [F] 24 D3
Hillegom [NL] 2 B4
Hilvarenbeek [NL] 6 B3
Hilversum [NL] 2 B4
Hirsingue [F] 28 E1
Hirson [F] 12 F2
Hochfelden [F] 22 E2
Hoedekenskerke [NL] 4 E3
Hoek van Holland [NL] 2 A4
Hohneck [F] 22 D3
Hohrodberg [F] 22 D3
Hollum [NL] 2 D1
Holten [NL] 2 D4
Holwerd [NL] 2 D2
Homps [F] 38 E2
Honfleur [F] 10 E2
Hoogerheide [NL] 4 F3
Hoogeveen [NL] 2 D3
Hoogezand [NL] 2 E2
Hoogkarspel [NL] 2 C3
Hoogstraten [B] 6 B3
Hoorn [NL] 2 B3
Hordain [F] 12 E1
Hornoy [F] 12 B2
Horst [B] 6 A4
Horst [NL] 6 C3
Hoscheid [L] 14 C3
Hospice de France [F] 36 F4
Hossegor [F] 30 A4
Hostens [F] 30 C3
Hotton [F] 14 B2
Houdan [F] 12 A4
Houdelaincourt [F] 20 E2
Houeillès [F] 30 D3
Houffalize [B] 14 C2
Houlgate [F] 10 E2
Hourtin [F] 24 B4
Hourtin-Plage [F] 24 A4
Hucqueliers [F] 4 B4
Huelgoat [F] 8 C3
Huizen [NL] 2 B3
Huizen [NL] 2 C4
Hulst [NL] 4 E3
Hunaudaye, Château de- [F] 8 E3
Hunspach [F] 22 E2
Huriel [F] 26 C3
Huy [B] 14 B1
Hyères [F] 40 F4

I

Ichtratzheim [F] 22 E3
Ieper (Ypres) [B] 4 D4
If, Château d'- [F] 40 E3
IJmuiden [NL] 2 B3
Illiers [F] 18 D1
Illiers-Combray [F] 18 D1
Imphy [F] 26 D4
Ingelmunster [B] 4 D4
Ingwiller [F] 22 E2
Isdes [F] 18 E3
Isigny-sur-Mer [F] 10 C2
Isola [F] 42 C2
Isola 2000 [F] 42 C2
Issoire [F] 32 E1
Issoudun [F] 26 B1
Is-sur-Tille [F] 20 D4
Istres [F] 40 D3
Isturits et d'Oxocelhaya, Grottes d'- [F] 36 C2
Itxassou [F] 36 C2
Ivry-la-Bataille [F] 12 A4
Izegem [B] 4 D4
Izernore [F] 28 B4

J

Jaligny-sur-Besbre [F] 26 D3
Janville [F] 18 E2
Janzé [F] 16 E1
Jard-sur-Mer [F] 24 A1
Jargeau [F] 18 E3
Jarnac [F] 24 C3
Jarnages [F] 26 B3
Jarny [F] 14 B4
Jaubrun [F] 32 D3
Jauge [F] 30 C2
Jausiers [F] 42 C1
Javron [F] 10 D4
Jeumont [F] 12 F1
Joigny [F] 20 B3
Joinville [F] 20 E2
Jonas, Grottes de- [F] 32 E1
Joncy [F] 26 F3
Jonzac [F] 24 C4
Josselin [F] 16 C1
Jouarre [F] 12 D4
Jougne [F] 28 D3
Joure [NL] 2 D2
Jovaic [F] 34 B4
Joyeuse [F] 32 F4
Juan-les-Pins [F] 42 C3
Jugon-les-Lacs [F] 8 E3
Juillac [F] 32 B1
Julliouville [F] 8 F4
Jumeaux [F] 32 E1
Jumièges [F] 10 F2
Juniville [F] 12 F3
Jussey [F] 20 F4
Juvigny-le-Tertre [F] 10 C3
Juzennecourt [F] 20 D3

K

Kaatsheuvel [NL] 6 B2
Kampen [NL] 2 D3
Kasterlee [B] 6 B3
Katwijk aan Zee [NL] 2 A4
Kaysersberg [F] 22 D3
Kerien [F] 8 D3
Kerjean, Château de- [F] 8 B2
Kernascléden [F] 8 C4
Kiriou, Roche de- [F] 8 C4
Klazienaveen [NL] 2 E3
Klerken [B] 4 D3
Knokke-Heist [B] 4 D3
Koetschette [L] 14 C3
Koksijde-Bad [B] 4 C3
Korrigans [F] 16 C2
Kortrijk (Courtrai) [B] 4 D4
Kotten [NL] 6 E2
Krimpen aan den IJssel [NL] 6 B2
Kruiningen [NL] 4 E3
Kruisland [NL] 4 F3

L

Laàs [F] 36 D2
la Balme [F] 34 C3
la Bastide [F] 42 B2

Labastide-d'Armagnac [F] 30 D3
La Bastide de-Sérou [F] 38 C3
Labastide-Murat [F] 32 B3
La Bastide-Puylaurent [F] 32 F3
Labastide-Rouairoux [F] 38 E2
La Bastie d'Urfé [F] 34 A1
La Bâtie-Neuve [F] 34 D4
La Baule [F] 16 C2
La Bazoche-Gouet [F] 18 C2
la Bégude-de-Mazenc [F] 34 B4
La Belle Etoile [F] 20 C2
Labenne [F] 30 A4
La Bérarde [F] 34 E3
L'Aber-Wrac'h [F] 8 B2
Laborel [F] 40 E1
Labouheyre [F] 30 B3
La Bourboule [F] 32 D1
Labrède [F] 30 C2
La Bresse [F] 22 D3
La Brillanne [F] 40 F2
Labrit [F] 30 C3
La Caillere-St-Hilaire [F] 24 C1
Lacalm [F] 32 D3
Lacanau [F] 30 C1
Lacanau-Océan [F] 30 B1
La Canonica [F] 44 C2
La Canourgue [F] 32 D4
La Capelle [F] 12 E2
Lacapelle-Marival [F] 32 B3
La Capte [F] 40 F4
Lacaune [F] 38 E1
La Cavalerie [F] 38 F1
Lacave [F] 32 B2
La Celle-Dunoise [F] 26 A3
La Chaise-Dieu [F] 32 F2
La Chambre [F] 34 E2
Lachamp [F] 32 E3
La Chapelle [F] 26 F4
La Chapelle-d'Angillon [F] 18 E4
la Chapelle-en-Valgaudemar [F] 34 D3
La Chapelle-en-Vercors [F] 34 C3
La Chapelle-Glain [F] 16 E2
la-Chapelle-Laurent [F] 32 E2
La Charité-sur-Loire [F] 26 D1
La Chartre-Sur-Le-Loir [F] 18 C2
La Châtaigneraie [F] 24 C1
La Châtre [F] 26 B2
la Chèze [F] 8 D4
La Ciotat [F] 40 E3
La Clayette [F] 26 E3
la Clisse [F] 24 B3
La Clusaz [F] 34 E1
La Cluse [F] 28 B4
La Cluse-et-Mijoux [F] 28 D3
La Coquille [F] 24 E4
La Corrèze [F] 32 C1
La Côte-St-André [F] 34 C2
Lacourt [F] 38 B3
La Courtine [F] 26 B4
la Couvertoirade [F] 38 F1
Lacq [F] 36 D2
La Croisière [F] 24 F3
La Croixille [F] 16 E1
La Croix-Valmer [F] 42 B4
La Cure [F] 28 C3
Ladapeyre [F] 26 B3
Ladon [F] 18 F2
Ladoye, Cirque de- [F] 28 C3

La Fère [F] 12 D3
La Ferrière [F] 34 D2
la Ferrière [F] 18 C3
La Ferrière-en-Parthenay [F] 24 D1
Laferté [F] 20 E4
La Ferté-Bernard [F] 18 C2
La Ferté-Gaucher [F] 20 B1
la-Française [F] 20 B3
La Ferté-Macé [F] 10 D4
La Ferté-Milon [F] 12 D3
La Ferté-sous-Jouarre [F] 12 D4
La Ferté-St-Aubin [F] 18 E3
La Ferté-Vidame [F] 10 F4
Laffrey [F] 34 D3
La Flèche [F] 18 B2
La Flotte [F] 24 B2
Lafrançaise [F] 30 F4
La Gacilly [F] 16 D1
La Garde-Freinet [F] 42 B3
Lagnieu [F] 34 C1
Lagny [F] 12 C4
Le Grand-Combe [F] 32 F4
La Grande-Motte [F] 40 C2
Lagrasse [F] 38 E3
La Grave [F] 34 E3
Laguépie [F] 32 B4
La Guerche [F] 26 C2
La Guerche-de-Bretagne [F] 16 E1
Laguiole [F] 32 D3
Lahane [F] 30 B3
la Haye [F] 12 E2
La Haye-du-Puits [F] 10 B2
Laheycourt [F] 20 E2
La Hutte [F] 18 B1
Laifour, Roches de- [F] 14 A2
L'Aigle [F] 10 E4
Laignes [F] 20 C3
L'Aiguillon [F] 24 B2
Laissac [F] 32 D4
la-Jaille-Yvon [F] 16 F2
La Javie [F] 42 B2
Lalinde [F] 30 E2
La Loupe [F] 18 D1
Lalouvesc [F] 34 B2
La Louvière [B] 12 F1
L'Alpe-d'Huez [F] 34 D3
La Machine [F] 26 D2
La Malène [F] 32 E4
Lamalou-les-Bains [F] 38 F2
Lamarche [F] 20 F3
Lamargelle [F] 20 D4
Lamarque [F] 30 C1
Lamastre [F] 34 B3
La Maucarrière [F] 16 F4
Lamballe [F] 8 E3
Lambesc [F] 40 E2
la-Melleraye-de-Bretagne [F] 16 E2
La Mongie [F] 36 E3
La Mothe-Achard [F] 16 D4
Lamotte-Beuvron [F] 18 E3
La Motte-Chalancon [F] 34 C4
la Motte-du-Caire [F] 40 F1
Lamouroux, Grottes de- [F] 32 B2
Lampaul [F] 8 A2
Lampaul-Plouarzel [F] 8 A2
La Mure [F] 34 D3
Lamure-sur-Azergues [F] 26 F4
La Napoule-Plage [F] 42 C3
Landerneau [F] 8 B3
Landévennec [F] 8 B3
Landivisiau [F] 8 B3
Landivy [F] 10 C4
Landrecies [F] 12 E2
La Neuve-Lyre [F] 10 F3

Langeac [F] 32 E2
Langeais [F] 18 B3
Langogne [F] 32 F3
Langoiran [F] 30 D2
Langon [F] 30 D2
Langres [F] 20 E3
Languidou, Chapelle de– [F] 8 B4
Lanleff, Temple de– [F] 8 D3
Lanmeur [F] 8 C2
Lannemezan [F] 36 E3
Lannilis [F] 8 B2
Lannion [F] 8 C2
Lanobre [F] 32 D1
Lanouaille [F] 32 B1
Lanslebourg-Mont-Cenis [F] 34 F3
Lantosque [F] 42 C2
Lanvollon [F] 8 D3
Laon [F] 12 E3
La Pacaudière [F] 26 E3
Lapalisse [F] 26 D3
La Pallice [F] 24 B2
Lapalme [F] 38 E3
La Palmyre [F] 24 B3
La Palud-sur-Verdon [F] 42 B2
la Panouse [F] 32 E3
la Péruse [F] 24 E3
La Petite-Pierre [F] 22 D2
Lapeyrade [F] 30 D3
La Plagne [F] 34 F2
Laplume [F] 30 E3
Lapoutroie [F] 22 D3
Laqueuille [F] 32 D1
Laragne-Montéglin [F] 40 F1
l'Arbre [F] 24 D3

L'Arbresle [F] 34 B1
Larceveau-Arros-Cibits [F] 36 C2
Larche [F] 32 B2
Larche [F] 42 C1
La Réole [F] 30 D2
Largentière [F] 34 A4
L'Argentière-la-Bessée [F] 34 E4
L'Armellière [F] 40 D2
Larmor [F] 16 B1
La Roche-Bernard [F] 16 C2
La Roche-Chalais [F] 30 D1
la Roche-de-Rame [F] 34 E4
La Roche-en-Ardenne [B] 14 B2
La Rochefoucauld [F] 24 D3
La Rochelle [F] 24 B2
La Roche-Posay [F] 24 E1
La Roche-sur-Foron [F] 28 C4
La Roche-sur-Yon [F] 16 D4
La Rochette [F] 34 D2
Larochette [L] 14 C3
Laroquebrou [F] 32 C2
La Roquebrussanne [F] 40 F3
Laroque-des-Arcs [F] 32 B3
Laroque-d'Olmes [F] 38 C3
La Roque-Gageac [F] 30 F2
La Rouche-Courbon [F] 24 B3
Larrau [F] 36 C3
Larret [F] 20 E4
Larroque [F] 32 B4
l'Artigue [F] 38 B3
Laruns [F] 36 D3
la Salles-les Alpes [F] 34 E3

La Salvetat [F] 32 C4
La Salvetat-sur-Agout [F] 38 E2
Lascaux, Grotte de– [F] 32 A2
la Selve [F] 32 C4
La Seyne [F] 40 E4
La Souterraine [F] 24 F3
Lassay [F] 10 C4
Lassigny [F] 12 D3
La Suze-sur-Sarthe [F] 18 B2
la Tannière [F] 10 C4
La Tour-du-Pin [F] 34 C2
La Tranche-sur-Mer [F] 24 B1
La Tremblade [F] 24 B3
La Trimouille [F] 24 F2
La Trinité [F] 16 B1
La Trinité-Porhoët [F] 8 D4
Latronquière [F] 32 C2
Latte, Fort la– [F] 8 E3
La Turbie [F] 42 D3
Laubrières [F] 16 E1
Laugratte [F] 30 E2
Laurière [F] 24 F3
Lauterbourg [F] 22 F2
Lautrec [F] 38 D1
Lauwersoog [NL] 2 D2
Lauzerte [F] 30 F3
Lauzun [F] 30 E2
Laval [F] 16 F1
Lavardac [F] 30 D3
Lavardin [F] 18 C2
Lavaur [F] 38 C1
Lavelanet [F] 38 C3
la Veurdre [F] 26 D2

Lavit [F] 30 E4
La Voulte-sur-Rhône [F] 34 B3
Lavoûte-Chilhac [F] 32 E2
Lavoûte-Polignac, Château de– [F] 32 F2
Lavoûte-sur-Loire [F] 32 F2
Lavoye [F] 20 E1
La Wantzenau [F] 22 E2
Le Bar [F] 42 C3
Le Barp [F] 30 C2
Le Beausset [F] 40 E3
Le Blanc [F] 24 F2
Le Boréon [F] 42 C2
Le Boulou [F] 38 E4
Le Bourg d'Oisans [F] 34 D3
Le Bourget [F] 34 D2
Le Bousquet-d'Orb [F] 38 F2
Le Bugue [F] 30 F2
le Caloy [F] 30 C3
Le Cap-d'Agde [F] 38 F3
Le Cateau-Cambrésis [F] 12 E2
Le Catelet [F] 12 D2
Le Caylar [F] 38 F1
L'Echalp [F] 34 F4
le Chambon-sur-Lignon [F] 34 A3
Le Chateau-d'Oléron [F] 24 B3
Le Châtelard [F] 34 E2
Le Châtelet [F] 26 B2
Le Chesne [F] 14 A3
Le Cheylard [F] 34 B3
Le Conquet [F] 8 A3
Le Coteau [F] 26 E4

Le Creusot [F] 26 F2
Le Croisic [F] 16 C2
Le Crotoy [F] 12 B1
Lectoure [F] 30 E4
Lédignan [F] 40 C1
Le Donjon [F] 26 E3
Le Dorat [F] 24 E3
Leek [NL] 2 D2
Leens [NL] 2 D2
Leerdam [NL] 6 B2
Leeuwarden [NL] 2 D2
Le Faou [F] 8 B3
Le Faouët [F] 8 C4
le Fayet [F] 34 E1
le Folgoet [F] 8 B2
Le Fossat [F] 38 C2
Le Freney [F] 34 E3
Le Fuilet [F] 16 E3
Legé [F] 16 D3
le Gouray [F] 8 E3
Le Grand-Bourg [F] 26 A3
Le Grand-Lucé [F] 18 C2
Le Grand-Pressigny [F] 18 C4
Le Grau-du-Roi [F] 40 C2
le Gressier [F] 30 B1
Léguevin [F] 38 B1
Le Havre [F] 10 E2
Le Hohwald [F] 22 D3
Leiden [NL] 2 A4
Le Lauzet-Ubaye [F] 42 B1
Le Lavandou [F] 42 B4
Le Lion-d'Angers [F] 16 F2
Le Logis-du-Pin [F] 42 B2
Le Loroux-Bottereau [F] 16 E3
Le Louroux [F] 16 E2
Le Luc [F] 42 B3
Le Ludd [F] 18 B2
Lelystad [NL] 2 C3
Le Mans [F] 18 B2
Le Markstein [F] 22 D4
Le Mas-d'Azil [F] 38 B2
Le Mayet [F] 26 D3
Lembach [F] 22 E1
Lembeye [F] 36 E2
Le Merlerault [F] 10 E4
Lemmer [NL] 2 C3
Le Monastier [F] 32 F3
Le Monêtier-les-Bains [F] 34 E3
Le Mont-Dore [F] 32 D1
Le Montet [F] 26 C3
Le Mont-St-Michel [F] 8 F3
Lempdes [F] 32 E2
Lempdes [F] 26 C4
le Mulins [F] 26 E4
Le Muret [F] 30 C2
Le Muy [F] 42 B3
Lencloître [F] 24 E1
Lencouacq [F] 30 C3
Le Neubourg [F] 10 F3
Léning [F] 22 D2
Le Nouvion-en-Thiérache [F] 12 E2
Lens [F] 12 D1
Léon [F] 30 B3
Leopoldsburg [B] 6 B4
Le Palais [F] 16 B2
L'Epau, Abbaye de– [F] 18 B2
Le-Péage-de-Roussillon [F] 34 B2
Le Perthus [F] 38 E4
Le Pin-au-Haras [F] 10 E4
l'Epine [F] 20 D1
le Plevnet [F] 34 D3
Le Poiré-sur-Vie [F] 16 D4
Le Pont-de-Beauvoisin [F] 34 D2
Le Pont-de-Claix [F] 34 D3

le Pont-de-Montvert [F] 32 E4
Le Pontet [F] 24 B4
Le Portel [F] 4 B4
Le Pouldu [F] 16 B1
Le Pouzin [F] 34 B3
Le Puy [F] 32 F2
Le Puy-en-Velay [F] 32 F2
Leques, Col des- [F] 42 B2
Le Quesnoy [F] 12 E1
Le Rabot [F] 18 E3
Le Rozier [F] 32 D4
Le Russey [F] 28 D2
Les Abrets [F] 34 D2
Les Adrets [F] 42 C3
Les Aix-d'Angillon [F] 18 E4
les Aldudes [F] 36 B2
Les Andelys [F] 12 A3
Les Antiques [F] 40 D2
Les Arcs [F] 34 F2
Les Arcs [F] 42 B3
Les Baux-de-Provence [F] 40 D2
Les Boulay Lue [F] 22 C1
Les Cabannes [F] 38 C3
Lescar [F] 36 D2
L'Escarène [F] 42 D2
Les Contamines-Montjoie [F] 34 E1
Les Deux-Alpes [F] 34 D3
Lesdins [F] 12 D2
Les Echarmeaux [F] 26 E4
Les Echelles [F] 34 D2
Les Epesses [F] 16 E4
Les Essarts [F] 16 D4
Les Eyzies-de-Tayac [F] 30 F2
Les Gets [F] 28 D4
Les Halles [F] 34 B1
Les Hayons [F] 12 A2
Les Herbiers [F] 16 E4
Les Houches [F] 34 F1
Les Issambres [F] 42 B3
Les Laumes [F] 20 C4
Les Lecques [F] 40 E3
Les Menuires [F] 34 E2
Lesmont [F] 20 D2
Lesneven [F] 8 B2
Lesparre-Médoc [F] 24 B4
Lesperon [F] 30 B3
Les Pieux [F] 10 B1
Les Planches-en-Montagne [F] 28 C3
Les Ponts-de-Cé [F] 16 F3
Les Riceys [F] 20 C3
Les Rosiers [F] 18 A3
Les Rousses [F] 28 C3
Les Sables-d'Olonne [F] 16 C4
Les Salles [F] 26 D4
Lessay [F] 10 B2
Lestards [F] 32 C1
Lestelle Bétharram [F] 36 D3
Les Trois-Epis [F] 22 D3
Les Trois-Moutiers [F] 18 A4
Les Vans [F] 32 F4
Le Teil [F] 34 B4
Le Teilleul [F] 10 C4
le Temple [F] 30 C1
Le Thillot [F] 22 C4
Le Touquet-Paris-Plage [F] 4 B4
Le Touvet [F] 34 D2
Le Trayas [F] 42 C3
Le Tréport [F] 12 B1
Leucate [F] 38 E3
Leuglay [F] 20 D3
Leuven (Louvain) [B] 6 A4
Le Val-André [F] 8 E3
Le Vaudreuil [F] 12 A3
Levens [F] 42 C2

Le Verdon [F] 24 B3
Le Vernet [F] 42 B1
Levet [F] 26 C2
Levie [F] 44 B3
Levier [F] 28 C2
Le Vigan [F] 40 B1
Levroux [F] 26 A1
Lézardrieux [F] 8 D2
Lézat [F] 28 C3
Lezay [F] 24 D2
Lézignan-Corbières [F] 38 E3
Lezoux [F] 26 D4
l'Hospitalet-l'Andorre [F] 38 C3
Libourne [F] 30 D1
Libramont [B] 14 B2
Lichtenberg [F] 22 E2
Lichtenvoorde [NL] 6 D2
Licques [F] 4 B4
Liège (Luik) [B] 14 B1
Lier [B] 4 F4
Liernais [F] 26 F1
Liesse [F] 12 E3
Lieu-Restauré, Abbaye de- [F] 12 D3
Lieurey [F] 10 E3
Liffré [F] 8 F4
Ligneuville [B] 14 C2
Lignières [F] 26 B2
Ligny-en-Barrois [F] 20 E2
Ligueil [F] 18 C4
Ligugé, Abbaye de- [F] 24 D2
Lillebonne [F] 10 F2
Limbourg [B] 14 C1
Limoges [F] 24 F3
Limogne-en-Quercy [F] 32 B3
Limonest [F] 34 B1
Limours [F] 18 E1
Limoux [F] 38 D3
Lipsheim [F] 22 E3
Lisieux [F] 10 E3
Lisle [F] 30 D1
L'Isle-Adam [F] 12 B3
L'Isle-de-Noé [F] 36 F2
L'Isle-en-Dodon [F] 38 B2
L'Isle-Jourdain [F] 38 B1
L'Isle-Jourdain [F] 24 E2
L'Isle-sur-la-Sorgue [F] 40 D2
L'Isle-sur-le-Doubs [F] 28 D1
Lisle-sur-Tarn [F] 38 D1
Lison, Source du- [F] 28 C2
Lisse [NL] 2 B4
Lit-et-Mixe [F] 30 B3
Livarot [F] 10 E3
Livernon [F] 32 B3
Livron [F] 34 B3
Livron-Sur-Drôme [F] 34 B3
Lizy [F] 12 D4
Llivia [F] 38 C4
L'Ile-Bouchard [F] 18 B4
L'Ile-Rousse [F] 44 B1
Lochem [NL] 6 D2
Loches [F] 18 C4
Locmaria [F] 16 B2
Locmariaquer [F] 16 B2
Locminé [F] 16 C1
Locquirec [F] 8 C2
Locronan [F] 8 B3
Loctudy [F] 8 B4
Lodève [F] 38 F2
Lohéac [F] 16 D1
Loire, Gorges de la- [F] 32 F3
Loisirs, Parc de- [F] 30 B2
Lokeren [B] 4 E3
Lombez [F] 38 B1

Lombrives, Grotte de- [F] 38 C3
Lomme [F] 4 D4
Lommel [B] 6 B3
Londinières [F] 12 B2
Longeau [F] 20 E4
Longeville les St. Avold [F] 22 C1
Longny-au-Perche [F] 10 E4
Longpont [F] 12 D3
Longué [F] 18 A3
Longueau [F] 12 C2
Longuyon [F] 14 B3
Longwy [F] 14 B3
Lons-le-Saunier [F] 28 B3
Looberghe [F] 4 C3
Loqueffret [F] 8 C3
Lorcé [B] 14 C1
Lorentzen [F] 22 D1
Lorgues [F] 42 B3
Lorient [F] 16 B1
Loriol-sur-Drôme [F] 34 B3
Lorlanges [F] 32 E2
Lormes [F] 26 E1
Lormont [F] 30 C1
Lorris [F] 18 F3
l'Ospedale [F] 44 B4
Losse [F] 30 D3
Loudéac [F] 8 D4
Loudes [F] 32 F2
Loudun [F] 18 A4
Loué [F] 18 B2
Loue, Source de la- [F] 28 D2
Louhans [F] 28 B3
Loulay [F] 24 C2
Louppy-sur-Loison [F] 14 B3
Lourdes [F] 36 E3
Loury [F] 18 E2
Louvain (Leuven) [B] 6 A4
Louvie-Juzon [F] 36 D3
Louviers [F] 12 A3
Lozari [F] 44 B1
Lubersac [F] 32 B1
Lucenay [F] 26 F2
Luc-en-Diois [F] 34 C4
Luçon [F] 24 B1
Luc-sur-Mer [F] 10 D2
Luigny [F] 18 D1
Luik (Liège) [B] 14 B1
Lumbres [F] 4 B4
Lummen [B] 6 B4
Lunas [F] 38 F2
Lunel [F] 40 C2
Lunéville [F] 22 C2
Lupiac [F] 30 D4
Lurcy-Lévis [F] 26 C2
Lure [F] 22 C4
Lureuil [F] 24 F1
Luri [F] 44 C1
Lusignan [F] 24 D2
Lusigny [F] 20 C2
Lus-la-Croix-Haute [F] 34 D4
Lussac-les-Châteaux [F] 24 E2
Lussac-les-Églises [F] 24 F2
Lussan [F] 40 C1
Lux [F] 28 A2
Luxembourg [L] 14 C3
Luxeuil-les-Bains [F] 22 C4
Luxey [F] 30 C3
Luzarches [F] 12 C3
Luzeret [F] 24 F2
Luz-St-Sauveur [F] 36 E3
Luzy [F] 26 E2
Lyon [F] 34 C1
Lyons-la-Forêt [F] 12 A3

M

Maaseik [B] 6 C4
Maasmechelen [B] 6 C4
Maassluis [NL] 4 F2
Machault [F] 12 F3
Mâchecourt [F] 16 D3
Macinaggio [F] 44 C1
Mâcon [F] 26 F3
Made [NL] 6 B2
Magescq [F] 30 B3
Magnac-Laval [F] 24 F3
Magneux Hte Rive [F] 34 A1
Magnières [F] 22 C2
Magny-Cours [F] 26 D2
Magny-en-Vexin [F] 12 B3
Magny-Jobert [F] 22 C4
Maguelone [F] 40 B2
Maîche [F] 28 D2
Maillezais [F] 24 C2
Mailly-le-Camp [F] 20 C1
Maintenon [F] 18 D1
Maison-Neuve [F] 20 D2
Malaucène [F] 40 E1
Malbouzon [F] 32 D3
Malbuisson [F] 28 D3
Maldegem [B] 4 E3
Malesherbes [F] 18 F2
Malestroit [F] 16 C1
Malfourat, Mine de- [F] 30 E2
Malicorne [F] 18 B2
Malines (Mechelen) [B] 4 F4
Malmédy [B] 14 C2
Malo-les-Bains [F] 4 C3
Maltat [F] 26 E2
Mamers [F] 18 C1
Mancier [F] 30 D4
Mandelieu [F] 42 C3
Mano [F] 30 C2
Manosque [F] 40 E2
Mansle [F] 24 D3
Manso [F] 44 B2
Mantes [F] 12 B3
Manzat [F] 26 C4
Marans [F] 24 B2
Marboz [F] 28 B3
Marchaux [F] 28 C2
Marche-en-Famenne [B] 14 B2
Marcheprime [F] 30 C2
Marciac [F] 36 E2
Marcigny [F] 26 E3
Marcillac-Vallon [F] 32 C3
Marcillat [F] 26 C3
Marcilly-le-Hayer [F] 20 B2
Marckolsheim [F] 22 E3
Marennes [F] 24 B3
Mareuil [F] 24 D4
Mareuil [F] 24 B1
Marhet [B] 14 B2
Mariémont [B] 12 F1
Marignane [F] 40 D3
Marigny-le-Châtel [F] 20 C2
Marine de Sisco [F] 44 C1
Marines [F] 12 B3
Maringues [F] 26 C4
Marle [F] 12 E2
Marlenheim [F] 22 E2
Marlens [F] 34 E1
Marmande [F] 30 D2
Marmoutier [F] 22 D2
Marnay [F] 28 C2
Marquion [F] 12 D1
Marquise [F] 4 B3
Marseillan [F] 38 F2
Marseillan-Plage [F] 38 F3
Marseille [F] 40 E3

Marseille-en-Beauvaisis [F] 12 B2
Martel [F] 32 B2
Martelange [B] 14 B3
Marthon [F] 24 D4
Martigné-Ferchaud [F] 16 E2
Martigues [F] 40 D3
Marvejols [F] 32 E3
Mas d'Azil, Grotte du- [F] 38 B2
Masevaux [F] 22 D4
Massat [F] 38 B3
Massay [F] 18 D4
Masseret [F] 24 F4
Masseube [F] 36 F2
Massiac [F] 32 E2
Mas Thibert [F] 40 D2
Matha [F] 24 C3
Mathay [F] 28 D1
Matignon [F] 8 E3
Matour [F] 26 F3
Maubeuge [F] 12 E1
Maubourguet [F] 36 E2
Mauléon [F] 16 E4
Mauléon-Licharre [F] 36 C2
Maulévrier [F] 16 E3
Maupas, Château de- [F] 18 E4
Maupertus-sur-Mer [F] 10 C1
Maure [F] 16 D1
Mauriac [F] 32 C2
Mauron [F] 8 E4
Maurs [F] 32 C3
Maury [F] 38 D3
Mauvezin [F] 38 B1
Mauzé-sur-le-Mignon [F] 24 C2
Mayenne [F] 10 C4
Mayet [F] 18 B2
Mazamet [F] 38 D2
Mazères [F] 38 C2
Mazerulles [F] 22 C2
Méandre de Queuille [F] 26 C4
Meaux [F] 12 C4
Mechelen (Malines) [B] 4 F4
Medemblik [NL] 2 C3
Médous, Grotte de- [F] 36 E3
Meeuwen [B] 6 C4
Megève [F] 34 E1
Mehun-sur-Yèvre [F] 18 E4
Meijel [NL] 6 C3
Meillant, Château de- [F] 26 C2
Meilleraye, Abbaye de- [F] 16 E2
Mélisey [F] 22 C4
Melle [F] 24 D2
Melun [F] 18 F1
Menat [F] 26 C4
Mende [F] 32 E3
Menec [F] 16 B1
Menen [B] 4 D4
Ménez Hom [F] 8 B3
Mens [F] 34 D3
Menthon [F] 34 E1
Menton [F] 42 D3
Meppel [NL] 2 D3
Mer [F] 18 D3
Merdrignac [F] 8 E4
Méréville [F] 18 E2
Méribel [F] 34 E2
Méribel-les-Allues [F] 34 E2
Merle, Tours de- [F] 32 C2
Mersch [L] 14 C3
Méru [F] 12 B3
Mervans [F] 28 B2
Merville [F] 4 C4
Méry [F] 20 C2

Meschers–sur–Gironde [F] 24 B3
Meslay [F] 16 F2
Mesnil–Val [F] 12 B1
Mesvres [F] 26 E2
Metabief [F] 28 D3
Méteren [F] 4 C4
Mettet [B] 14 A1
Metz [F] 22 C1
Metzervisse [F] 14 C4
Meulan [F] 12 B3
Meung–sur–Loire [F] 18 D3
Meux [F] 14 A1
Meximieux [F] 34 C1
Meymac [F] 32 C1
Meyrargues [F] 40 E2
Meyrueis [F] 32 E4
Meyzieu [F] 34 C1
Mèze [F] 40 B2
Mézel [F] 42 B2
Mézières [F] 24 E3
Mézières–en–Brenne [F] 24 F1
Mézilhac [F] 34 A3
Mézin [F] 30 D3
Mèzos [F] 30 B3
Middelburg [NL] 4 E3
Middelharnis [NL] 4 F2
Middelkerke–Bad [B] 4 D3
Midsland [NL] 2 C1
Miélan [F] 36 E2
Migennes [F] 20 B3
Mijoux [F] 28 C4
Millas [F] 38 D4
Millau [F] 32 D4
Millevaches [F] 26 B4
Mimizan [F] 30 B3
Mimizan–Plage [F] 30 B3
Mindin [F] 16 C2
Minervio [F] 44 C1
Miramar [F] 42 C3
Miramas [F] 40 D2
Mirambeau [F] 24 B4
Miramont–de–Guyenne [F] 30 E2
Mirande [F] 36 F2
Mirebeau [F] 24 D1
Mirebeau [F] 28 B1
Mirecourt [F] 22 B3
Mirepoix [F] 38 C2
Modane [F] 34 E2
Modave [B] 14 B1
Moirans [F] 34 C2
Moirans–en–Montagne [F] 28 B3
Moissac [F] 30 F4
Mol [B] 6 B3
Molens Van Kinderdijk [NL] 6 B2
Molières [F] 30 F4
Molliens [F] 12 B2
Moloy [F] 20 D4
Molsheim [F] 22 E2
Monaco [MC] 42 D3
Moncontour [F] 8 D3
Moncoutant [F] 16 E4
Mondaye, Abbaye de– [F] 10 D2
Mondorf–les–Bains [L] 14 C4
Mondoubleau [F] 18 C2
Monestier–de–Clermont [F] 34 C3
Monêtier–Allemont [F] 40 F1
Monflanquin [F] 30 E3
Monistrol–d'Allier [F] 32 E2
Monistrol–sur–Loire [F] 34 A2
Monnickendam [NL] 2 B3
Monpazier [F] 30 F2
Monplaisir [F] 18 C2
Mons (Bergen) [B] 12 F1

Monségur [F] 30 D2
Montagnac [F] 38 F2
Montaigu [F] 16 D3
Montaigu–de–Quercy [F] 30 F3
Montaigut [F] 26 C3
Montalieu [F] 34 C1
Montalivet–les–Bains [F] 24 B4
Montaren [F] 40 C1
Montargis [F] 18 F3
Montastruc la–Conseillère [F] 38 C1
Montauban [F] 30 F4
Montauban [F] 8 E4
Montbard [F] 20 C4
Montbazens [F] 32 C3
Montbazon [F] 18 C3
Montbéliard [F] 28 D1
Montbenoît [F] 28 D2
Montbonnot [F] 34 D3
Montbrison [F] 34 A1
Montbron [F] 24 D4
Montbrun–les–Bains [F] 40 E1
Montceau–les–Mines [F] 26 F3
Montchanin [F] 26 F2
Montcornet [F] 12 E3
Montcuq [F] 30 F3
Mont–de–Marsan [F] 30 C3
Montdidier [F] 12 C2
Mont–Dol [F] 8 F3
Montebourg [F] 10 C2
Monte–Carlo [MC] 42 D3
Montech [F] 30 F4
Montel–de–Gelat [F] 26 B4
Montélimar [F] 34 B4
Montendre [F] 24 C4
Montereau–Faut–Yonne [F] 20 B2
Montereau [F] 18 F3
Montesquieu–Volvestre [F] 38 B2
Montesquiou [F] 36 F2
Montfaucon–en–Velay [F] 34 A2
Montferrat [F] 42 B3
Montfort [F] 8 E4
Montfort [F] 12 B4
Montfort–En–Chalosse [F] 30 B4
Mont Gargan [F] 24 F4
Montgenèvre [F] 34 E3
Montgeoffroy, Château de– [F] 18 A3
Montgiscard [F] 38 C2
Montguyon [F] 30 D1
Monthermé [F] 8 E4
Monthureaux–sur–Saône [F] 20 F3
Montier–en–Der [F] 20 D2
Montignac [F] 32 A2
Montigny–le–Roi [F] 20 E3
Montigny–sur–Aube [F] 20 D3
Montivilliers [F] 10 E2
Montlieu–la–Garde [F] 24 C4
Mont–Louis [F] 38 C4
Montluçon [F] 26 C3
Montluel [F] 34 C1
Montmajour, Abbaye de– [F] 40 D2
Montmarault [F] 26 C3
Montmédy [F] 14 B3
Montmélian [F] 34 D2
Montmeyan [F] 40 F3
Montmirail [F] 18 C2
Montmirail [F] 20 C1
Montmirey [F] 28 B2

Montmoreau–St–Cybard [F] 24 D4
Montmorillon [F] 24 E2
Montmort [F] 12 E4
Montoire–sur–le–Loir [F] 18 C2
Montoy–Flanville [F] 22 C1
Montpellier [F] 40 B2
Montpellier–Le–Vieux [F] 32 D4
Montpezat [F] 32 B3
Montpon–Ménestérol [F] 30 E1
Montpont–en–Bresse [F] 28 B3
Montréal [F] 30 D4
Montréal [F] 38 D2
Montréal [F] 20 C4
Montredon–Labessonnie [F] 38 D1
Montréjeau [F] 36 F3
Montrésor [F] 18 C4
Montret [F] 28 B3
Montreuil–aux–Lions [F] 12 D4
Montreuil–Bellay [F] 18 A3
Montrevault [F] 16 E3
Montrevel [F] 28 B3
Montrichard [F] 18 C3
Montrond–les–Bains [F] 34 B1
Montsalvy [F] 32 C3
Montsauche–les–Settons [F] 26 E1
Montségur [F] 38 C3
Montsoreau [F] 18 B3
Mont–sous–Vaudrey [F] 28 B2
Monts–s–Guesnes [F] 18 B4
Mont–Ste–Odile [F] 22 D3
Montsûrs [F] 18 A1
Monze [F] 38 D3
Morcenx [F] 30 B3
Mordelles [F] 16 D1
Moreno, Col de la– [F] 26 C4
Morestel [F] 34 C2
Moret–sur–Loing [F] 20 A2
Moreuil [F] 12 C2
Morez [F] 28 C4
Morgat [F] 8 B3
Morhange [F] 22 C1
Moriani–Plage [F] 44 C2
Morigny Champigny [F] 18 E1
Moriville [F] 22 C3
Morlaàs [F] 36 E2
Morlaix [F] 8 C3
Mormant [F] 20 A1
Mornay–Berry [F] 26 C1
Morosaglia [F] 44 C2
Mortagne–au–Perche [F] 10 E4
Mortagne–sur–Sèvre [F] 16 E4
Mortain [F] 10 C3
Morteau [F] 28 D2
Mortier–Crolle, Château de– [F] 16 F2
Mortrée [F] 10 D4
Morzine [F] 28 D4
Motte–Glain, Château de la– [F] 16 E2
Mouchard [F] 28 C2
Mougins [F] 42 C3
Mouliherne [F] 18 B3
Moulins [F] 26 D2
Moulins–Engilbert [F] 26 E2
Moulins–la–Marche [F] 10 E4
Moustiers–Ste–Marie [F] 42 B2

Mouthe [F] 28 C3
Mouthier [F] 28 D2
Mouthoumet [F] 38 D3
Moutier–d'Ahun [F] 26 B3
Moûtiers [F] 34 E2
Moutiers [F] 24 B1
Mouton–Rothschild [F] 24 B4
Mouy [F] 12 C3
Mouzon [F] 14 A3
Mt–Dauphin [F] 34 E4
Mugron [F] 30 C4
Mulhouse [F] 22 D4
Munster [F] 22 D3
Murat [F] 32 D2
Murato [F] 44 C2
Murat–sur–Vèbre [F] 38 E2
Mur–de–Barrez [F] 32 D3
Mur–de–Bretagne [F] 8 D4
Muret [F] 38 C2
Muro [F] 44 B2
Musselkanaal [NL] 2 E3
Mussidan [F] 30 E1
Mussy [F] 20 D3
Muzillac [F] 16 C2

N

Naarden [NL] 2 B4
Nadrin [B] 14 B2
Nailloux [F] 38 C2
Najac [F] 32 B4
Nalzen [F] 38 C3
Namur [B] 14 A1
Nancy [F] 22 C2
Nangis [F] 20 B1
Nans–les–Pins [F] 40 E3
Nant [F] 38 F1
Nantes [F] 16 D3
Nanteuil–le–Haudouin [F] 12 C3
Nantiat [F] 24 F3
Nantua [F] 28 B4
Naours, Grottes de– [F] 12 C1
Narbonne [F] 38 E3
Narbonne–Plage [F] 38 E3
Nasbinals [F] 32 D3
Navacelles, Cirque de– [F] 40 B1
Navarrenx [F] 36 D2
Navilly [F] 28 B2
N.–D. de Clausis [F] 34 F4
N.–D. de Kerdevot [F] 8 B4
N.–D. de la Salette [F] 34 D3
N.–D. de Lure [F] 40 F2
N.–D. de Miracles [F] 42 C3
N.–D.–du–Haut [F] 22 C4
N.–D. du Mai [F] 40 E4
Neauvic [F] 30 E1
Neede [NL] 6 D2
Négrondes [F] 30 F1
Nemours [F] 18 F2
Nérac [F] 30 D3
Néré [F] 24 C3
Néris–les–Bains [F] 26 C3
Néronde [F] 26 C1
Nes [NL] 2 D1
Nesle [F] 12 D2
Nettancourt [F] 20 E1
Neuf–Brisach [F] 22 E4
Neufchâteau [B] 14 B3
Neufchâteau [F] 20 F2
Neufchâtel [F] 12 E3
Neufchâtel–en–Bray [F] 12 B2
Neuillé Port–Pierre [F] 18 B3

Neuilly–l'Évêque [F] 20 E3
Neuilly–St–Front [F] 12 D4
Neu–Moresnet [B] 14 C1
Neung–sur–Beuvron [F] 18 D3
Neuves–Maisons [F] 22 C2
Neuvic [F] 32 C1
Neuville [F] 34 C1

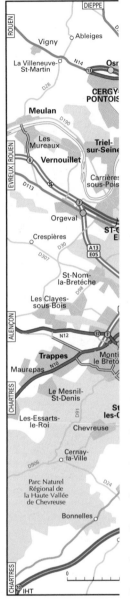

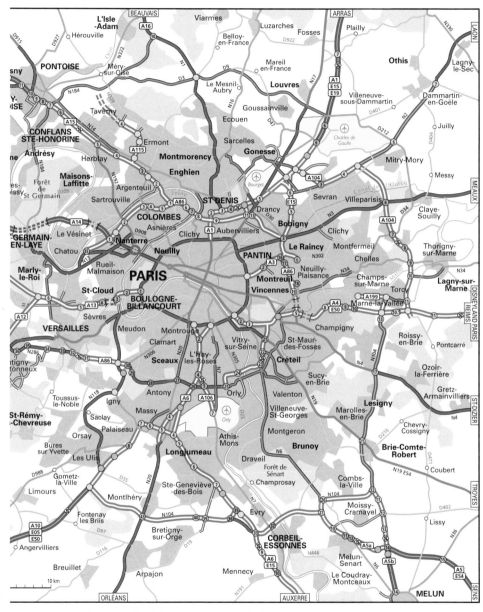

Neuville [F] 24 D1
Neuville-aux-Bois [F] 18 E2
Neuvy [F] 26 B2
Neuvy-Bouin [F] 24 C1
Neuvy-sur-Barangeon [F] 18 E4
Nevers [F] 26 D2
Nexon [F] 24 E4

Niaux, Grotte de– [F] 38 C3
Nice [F] 42 C3
Nideck, Château du– [F] 22 D2
Niederbronn-les-Bains [F] 22 E2
Nieppe [F] 4 D4
Nieuil [F] 24 D3

Nieuweschans [NL] 2 F2
Nieuwpoort [B] 4 D3
Nijkerk [NL] 2 C4
Nijmegen [NL] 6 C2
Nijverdal [NL] 2 D4
Nîmes [F] 40 C2
Ninove [B] 4 E4
Niort [F] 24 C2

Nitry [F] 20 C3
Nivelles [B] 12 F1
Niversac [F] 30 F1
Nizy–le-Comte [F] 12 E3
Noailles [F] 12 C3
Nods [F] 28 D2
Noé [F] 38 B2
Nogaro [F] 30 D4

Nogent [F] 20 E3
Nogent–le-Roi [F] 12 A4
Nogent-le-Rotrou [F] 18 C1
Nogent-sur-Seine [F] 20 B2
Noirétable [F] 26 D4
Noirmoutier–en–l'Île [F] 16 C3
Nolay [F] 26 F2

Nomeny [F] 22 C1
Nomexy [F] 22 C3
Nonancourt [F] 10 F4
Nonant-le-Pin [F] 10 E4
Nontron [F] 24 D4
Nonza [F] 44 C1
Noordwijk aan Zee [NL] 2 A4
Nordausques [F] 4 B4
Norg [NL] 2 E2
Nort-Sur-Erdre [F] 16 D2
Notre-Dame de Consolation
[F] 28 D2
Notre-Dame de-la-Roquette
[F] 42 B3
Notre-Dame des Fontaines
[F] 42 D2
Nouan-le-Fuzelier [F] 18 E3
Nouans-les-Fontaines [F] 18
C4
Nouvaillé-Maupertuis [F] 24
E2
Nouvion [F] 12 B1
Noves [F] 40 D2
Novion-Porcien [F] 12 F3
Noyant [F] 18 B3
Noyers [F] 20 C3
Noyers-sur-Jabron [F] 40 F1
Noyon [F] 12 D3
Nozay [F] 16 D2
Nozeroy [F] 28 C3
Nuits-St-Georges [F] 28 B2
Nunspeet [NL] 2 C4
Nyons [F] 34 B4

O

O, Château d'- [F] 10 D4
Obernai [F] 22 E3
Objat [F] 32 B1
Odoorn [NL] 2 E3
Oêtre, Roche d'- [F] 10 D3
Oiron [F] 18 A4
Oirschot [NL] 6 B3
Oisemont [F] 12 B1
Oissel [F] 12 A3
Oisterwijk [NL] 6 B3
Olargues [F] 38 E2
Oldeberkoop [NL] 2 D3
Oldenzaal [NL] 2 E4
Olen [B] 6 B4
Oletta [F] 44 C2
Olette [F] 38 D4
Olivet [F] 18 E3
Olliergues [F] 32 F1
Olmeto [F] 44 B3
Olonzac [F] 38 D2
Oloron-Ste-Marie [F] 36 D2
Olst [NL] 2 D4
Ommen [NL] 2 D3
Onnaing [F] 12 E1
Ooidonk [B] 4 E4
Oostburg [NL] 4 E3
Oostende [B] 4 D3
Oosterbeek [NL] 6 C2
Oostérend [NL] 2 C1
Oosterhout [NL] 6 B2
Oosterwolde [NL] 2 D2
Oostmalle [B] 6 A3
Ootmarsum [NL] 2 E4
Oploo [NL] 6 C3
Oppidum d'Ensérune [F] 38 E2
Oraison [F] 40 F2
Orange [F] 40 D1
Orasi [F] 44 B4
Orbec [F] 10 E3
Orbey [F] 22 D3

Orches [F] 18 B4
Orchies [F] 12 E1
Orcières [F] 34 E4
Orgelet [F] 28 B3
Orgeval [F] 12 B4
Orgnac-l'Aven [F] 34 A4
Orgon [F] 40 D2
Orléans [F] 18 E2
Orly [F] 12 C4
Ornans [F] 28 C2
Orthez [F] 36 D2
Orto [F] 44 B2
Ostwald [F] 22 E2
Otterlo [NL] 6 C2
Ouanne [F] 20 B3
Oucques [F] 18 D2
Oud Beijerland [NL] 6 A2
Ouddorp [NL] 4 F2
Oudenaarde [B] 4 E4
Oude-Pekela [NL] 2 E2
Oudewater [NL] 2 B4
Ouistreham [F] 10 D2
Oullins [F] 34 B1
Ourscamps, Abbaye d'- [F]
12 D3
Oust [F] 38 B3
Ouzouer-le-Marché [F] 18 D2
Oyonnax [F] 28 B4

P

Pacy-sur-Eure [F] 12 A3
Padirac, Gouffre de- [F] 32
B2
Pagny-Sur-Moselle [F] 22 C1
Pailhès [F] 38 C2
Paimboeuf [F] 16 D2
Paimpol [F] 8 D2
Paladru [F] 34 D2
Palaiseau [F] 12 B4
Palavas-les-Flots [F] 40 B2
Paliseul [F] 14 B2
Palluau [F] 16 D4
Pamiers [F] 38 C2
Panassac [F] 36 F2
Parata, Tour de la- [F] 44 A3
Paray-le-Monial [F] 26 E3
Parentis-en-Born [F] 30 B2
Pargny-sur-Saulx [F] 20 D1
Paris [F] 12 C4
Parisot [F] 32 B3
Parthenay [F] 24 D1
Partinello [F] 44 A2
Pas-en-Artois [F] 12 C1
Patay [F] 18 D2
Pau [F] 36 D2
Pauillac [F] 24 B4
Paulhaguet [F] 32 E2
Pavilly [F] 10 F2
Payrac [F] 32 B2
Péaule [F] 16 C2
Pech-Merle, Grotte du- [F]
32 B3
Peïra-Cava [F] 42 D2
Pellegrue [F] 30 D2
Pélussin [F] 34 B2
Pendus, Rocher des- [F] 32
D2
Penestin [F] 16 C2
Penmarch, Pointe de- [F] 8
B4
Pentrez-Plage [F] 8 B3
Percy [F] 10 C3
Père de Montfort, Grotte du-
[F] 24 C1

Périers [F] 10 C2
Pérignác [F] 24 C3
Périgueux [F] 30 F1
Perkpolder [NL] 4 E3
Pernes [F] 40 D2
Pernes-les-Fontaines [F] 40
D2
Peron [F] 28 C4
Péronne [F] 12 D2
Pérouges [F] 34 C1
Perpignan [F] 38 E4
Perros-Guirec [F] 8 C2
Pertuis [F] 40 E2
Péruwelz [B] 12 E1
Perwez [B] 14 A1
Pesmes [F] 28 C2
Pétange [L] 14 C3
Petreto-Bicchisano [F] 44 B3
Peyrat-le-Chateaux [F] 26
A4
Peyrehorade [F] 30 B4
Peyrolles [F] 40 E2
Peyruis [F] 40 F2
Peyrusse-le-Roc [F] 32 C3
Pézenas [F] 38 F2
Phalsbourg [F] 22 D2
Philippeville [B] 14 A2
Piana [F] 44 A2
Pianotolli-Caldarello [F] 44
D4
Picquigny [F] 12 C2
Piedicroce [F] 44 C2
Piennes [F] 14 B4
Pierre-Buffière [F] 24 F4
Pierre-de-Bresse [F] 28 B2
Pierrefitte [F] 20 E1
Pierrefitte-Nestalas [F] 36 E3
Pierrefonds [F] 12 D3
Pierrefort [F] 32 D2
Pierrefort, Château de- [F] 20
F1
Pierrelatte [F] 34 B4
Pierroton [F] 30 C2
Pietralba [F] 44 B2
Pilat, Dune de- [F] 30 B2
Pilat-Plage [F] 30 B2
Pinarellu [F] 44 B4
Piney [F] 20 D2
Pino [F] 44 C1
Pinols [F] 32 E2
Pionsat [F] 26 C4
Pipriac [F] 16 D1
Piriac-sur-Mer [F] 16 C2
Pirou-Plage [F] 10 B2
Pissos [F] 30 C3
Pithiviers [F] 18 E2
Plabennec [F] 8 B2
Plage de Pineto [F] 44 C2
Plaigne [F] 38 C2
Plaisance [F] 36 E2
Plancoët [F] 8 E3
Plan-du-Lac [F] 34 F1
Pleaux [F] 32 C2
Plélan-le-Grand [F] 16 D1
Plesse [F] 16 D2
Plessis-Bourré, Château du-
[F] 16 F2
Plestin-les-Grèves [F] 8 C2
Pleumartin [F] 24 E1
Pleyben [F] 8 B3
Ploërmel [F] 16 C1
Plombières-les-Bains [F] 22
C3
Plonéour Lanvern [F] 8 B4
Plouaret [F] 8 C3
Plouay [F] 8 C4
Ploubalay [F] 8 E3
Ploudalmézeau [F] 8 B2
Plouescat [F] 8 B2
Plougasnou [F] 8 C2
Plougastel-Daoulas [F] 8 B3

Plouguenast [F] 8 D4
Plouha [F] 8 D3
Plouigneau [F] 8 C3
Ploumanac'h [F] 8 C2
Plouray [F] 8 C4
Plozévet [F] 8 B4
Pluviers [F] 24 E4
Pluvigner [F] 16 B1
Podensac [F] 30 D2
Poeldijk [NL] 2 A4
Pointe des Poulains [F] 16
B2
Point Sublime [F] 32 D4
Poissons [F] 20 E2
Poitiers [F] 24 E2
Poix [F] 12 B2
Poligny [F] 28 C2
Pompey [F] 22 C2
Poncin [F] 28 B4
Pons [F] 24 C3
Pont [F] 28 B2
Pontacq [F] 36 E3
Pontailler-sur-Saône [F] 28
B2
Pont-à-Mousson [F] 22 C1
Pontarion [F] 26 A3
Pontarlier [F] 28 D2
Pontaubault [F] 10 B3
Pont-Audemer [F] 10 E2
Pontaumur [F] 26 C4
Pont-Aven [F] 8 B4
Pont Cellier [F] 26 C3
Pontcharra [F] 34 D2
Pontchartrain [F] 12 B4
Pontchâteau [F] 16 D2
Pont-Croix [F] 8 A3
Pont-d'Ain [F] 28 B4
Pont-de-Briques [F] 4 B4
Pont-de-Dore [F] 26 D4
Pont-de-l'Arche [F] 12 A3
Pont-de-Roide [F] 28 D2
Pont-de-Salars [F] 32 D4
Pont-d'Espagne [F] 36 D3
Pont-de-Vaux [F] 28 A3
Ponte-Leccia [F] 44 B2
Pont-en-Royans [F]
34 C3
Ponte Nuovo [F] 44 C2
Pontgibaud [F] 26 C4
Pontigny [F] 20 B3
Pontivy [F] 8 D4
Pont-l'Abbé [F] 8 B4
Pont-l'Évêque [F] 10 E2
Pontlevoy [F] 18 C3
Pontoise [F] 12 B3
Pontorson [F] 8 F3
Pontpierre [L] 14 C3
Pont-Réan [F] 16 D1
Pontrieux [F] 8 D3
Pont-Scorff [F] 8 C4
Pont-St-Esprit [F] 40 D1
Pont-St-Vincent [F] 22 C2
Pont-sur-Yonne [F] 20 B2
Pontvallain [F] 18 B2
Poperinge [B] 4 C4
Pornic [F] 16 C3
Pornichet [F] 16 C2
Porquerolles [F] 40 F4
Portbail [F] 10 B2
Port-Barcarès [F] 38 E3
Port-Camargue [F] 40 C2
Port-Cros [F] 42 B4
Port-de-Bouc [F] 40 D3
Port-en-Bessin [F] 10 D2
Portes les Valence [F] 34 B3
Port-Grimaud [F] 42 B3
Porticcio [F] 44 B3
Port-Joinville [F] 16 C4
Port-la-Nouvelle [F] 38 E3
Port-Leucate [F] 38 E3
Port-Louis [F] 16 B1

Port-Manech [F] 8 B4
Port-Navalo [F] 16 B2
Porto [F] 44 A2
Porto-Pollo [F] 44 B3
Porto-Vecchio [F] 44 B4
Port-Ste-Marie [F] 30 E3
Port-St-Louis-du-Rhône [F]
40 D3
Port-St-Marie, La Chartreuse
de- [F] 26 C4
Port-sur-Saône [F] 20 F4
Port-Vendres [F] 38 E4
Pouancé [F] 16 E2
Pougues-les-Eaux [F] 26 D1
Pouilly [F] 18 F4
Pouilly-en-Auxois [F] 26 F1
Pouilly-sous-Charlieu [F] 26
E4
Pouyastruc [F] 36 E3
Pouy-de-Touges [F] 38 B2
Pouzauges [F] 16 E4
Pradelle [F] 34 C4
Pradelles [F] 32 F3
Prades [F] 38 D4
Prahecq [F] 24 C2
Pralognan-la-Vanoise [F] 34
E2
Prats-de-Mollo-la-Preste
[F] 38 D4
Prauthoy [F] 20 E4
Préchac [F] 30 C3
Précy-sous-Thil [F] 20 C4
Precy Sur Vrin [F] 20 B3
Pré-en-Pail [F] 10 D4
Prémery [F] 26 D1
Prénouvellon [F] 18 D2
Pressac [F] 24 E3
Preuilly-sur-Claise [F] 24 F1
Préveranges [F] 26 B2
Primel-Trégastel [F] 8 C2
Prissac [F] 24 F2
Privas [F] 34 B3
Profondeville [B] 14 A1
Propriano [F] 44 B3
Prouille [F] 38 D2
Provins [F] 20 B1
Prunet [F] 32 C3
Prunete [F] 44 C2
Prunet-et-Belpuig [F] 38 D4
Puget-sur-Argens [F] 42 B3
Puget-Théniers [F] 42 C2
Puget-Ville [F] 40 F3
Puiseaux [F] 18 F2
Puivert [F] 38 D3
Punta, Château de la- [F] 44
A3
Purmerend [NL] 2 B3
Putanges-Pont-Ecrepin [F]
10 D3
Puttelange [F] 22 D1
Putten [NL] 2 C4
Puvvalador [F] 38 D3
Puy de Dôme [F] 26 C4
Puyguilhem [F] 24 E4
Puy-Guillaume [F] 26 D4
Puylaurens [F] 38 D2
Puy-l'Évêque [F] 30 F3
Puymorens, Col de- [F] 38
C4
Pyla-sur-Mer [F] 30 B2

Q

Quarré-les-Tombes [F] 20
C4
Qudeschild [NL] 2 B2

Quelaines–St. Gault [F] 16 F2
Quercamps [F] 4 B4
Québirus, Château de– [F] 38 D3
Quéroy, Grottes du– [F] 24 D4
Questembert [F] 16 C2
Quettehou [F] 10 C1
Quiberon [F] 16 B2
Quillan [F] 38 D3
Quimper [F] 8 B4
Quimperlé [F] 8 C4
Quinéville [F] 10 C1
Quingey [F] 28 C2
Quintin [F] 8 D3
Quissac [F] 40 C2

R

Raalte [NL] 2 D4
Rabastens [F] 38 C1
Rabastens–de–Bigorre [F] 36 E2
Rambervillers [F] 22 C3
Rambouillet [F] 18 E1
Randan [F] 26 D4
Rânes [F] 10 D4
Raon–l'Etape [F] 22 D3
Ravel [F] 26 D4
Raversijde [B] 4 D3
Rayol [F] 42 B4
Réalmont [F] 38 D1
Reau [F] 18 F1
Réau, Ancient Abbaye de la– [F] 24 E2
Rebais [F] 12 D4
Recey–sur–Ource [F] 20 D3
Recologne [F] 28 C2
Redon [F] 16 D2
Reichstett [F] 22 E2
Reignier [F] 28 C4
Reillanne [F] 40 E2
Reims [F] 12 E4
Rely [F] 4 C4
Rémalard [F] 18 C1
Remich [F] 14 C3
Remiremont [F] 22 C3
Remouchamps [B] 14 C1
Remoulins [F] 40 D2
Rémuzat [F] 34 C4
Renaison [F] 26 E4
Renaix (Ronse) [B] 4 E4
Renkum [NL] 6 C2
Rennes [F] 16 E1
République, Col de la– [F] 34 B2
Réquista [F] 32 C4
Ressons [F] 12 C3
Rethel [F] 12 F3
Retie [B] 6 B3
Retiers [F] 16 E1
Retournac [F] 32 F2
Reuilly [F] 18 E4
Reusel [NL] 6 B3
Revel [F] 38 D2
Révigny [F] 20 E1
Révigny–sur–Ornain [F] 20 E1
Revin [F] 14 A2
Rhenen [NL] 6 C2
Rhinau [F] 22 E3
Riaillé [F] 16 E2
Rians [F] 40 E3
Ribeauville [F] 22 D3
Ribécourt [F] 12 D3
Ribemont [F] 12 E2

Ribérac [F] 30 E1
Richelieu [F] 18 B4
Rieumes [F] 38 B2
Rieupeyroux [F] 32 C3
Rieussec [F] 38 E2
Rieux [F] 38 B2
Riez [F] 40 F2
Rignac [F] 32 C3
Rijssen [NL] 2 D4
Rillé [F] 18 B3
Riom [F] 26 C4
Riom–ès–Montagnes [F] 32 D2
Rion–des–Landes [F] 30 B3
Rioz [F] 28 C1
Riquewihr [F] 22 D3
Riscle [F] 30 C4
Riva–Bella [F] 10 D2
Rive–de–Gier [F] 34 B2
Rivesaltes [F] 38 E3
Roanne [F] 26 E4
Rocamadour [F] 32 B2
Rochebloine, Château de– [F] 34 B3
Rochechouart [F] 24 E3
Rochecourbière, Grotte de– [F] 34 B4
Rochefort [B] 14 B2
Rochefort [F] 24 B2
Rochefort, Grotte de– [F] 18 A2
Rochefort–en–Terre [F] 16 C1
Rochefort–s–Nenon [F] 28 B2
Rochehaut [B] 14 A3
Rochemaure [F] 34 B4
Rocher, Château du– [F] 18 A1
Rocherolle, Château de la– [F] 26 A2
Rochers, Château des– [F] 16 E1
Rocheservière [F] 16 D3
Rocroi [F] 12 F2
Rodange [L] 14 B3
Roden [NL] 2 D2
Rodez [F] 32 C3
Roermond [NL] 6 C4
Roesulare (Roulers) [B] 4 D4
Roeulx [B] 12 F1
Rogliano [F] 44 C1
Rognac [F] 40 D3
Rohan [F] 8 D4
Rohrbach–lès–Bitche [F] 22 D1
Roisel [F] 12 D2
Romans–sur–Isère [F] 34 C3
Rombas [F] 14 C4
Romilly–sur–Seine [F] 20 C2
Romorantin–Lanthenay [F] 18 D4
Ronchamp [F] 22 C4
Ronse (Renaix) [B] 4 E4
Roodeschool [NL] 2 E2
Roosendaal [NL] 4 F3
Roque, Pointe de la– [F] 10 E2
Roquebillière [F] 42 D2
Roquebrune–Cap–Martin [F] 42 D3
Roquefort [F] 30 C3
Roquefort–sur–Soulzon [F] 38 F1
Roquemaure [F] 40 D1
Roquesteron [F] 42 C2
Roquetaillade, Château de– [F] 30 D2
Rosans [F] 34 C4
Roscoff [F] 8 C2
Rosporden [F] 8 B4
Rostassac [F] 30 F3

Rostrenen [F] 8 C3
Rothéneuf [F] 8 F3
Rotterdam [NL] 6 A2
Roubaix [F] 4 D4
Rouen [F] 12 A2
Rouffach [F] 22 D4
Rouffignac, Grotte de– [F] 30 F2
Rougé [F] 16 E2
Rougemont [F] 28 D1
Rougemont [F] 22 D4
Rouillac [F] 24 C3
Roujan [F] 38 F2
Roulers (Roeselare) [B] 4 D4
Roussillon [F] 40 E2
Rouvres–en–Xaintois [F] 20 F3
Royan [F] 24 B3
Royat [F] 26 C4
Royaumont, Abbaye de– [F] 12 C3
Roybon [F] 34 C2
Roye [F] 12 D2
Royère–de–Vassivière [F] 26 A4
Rozay–en–Brie [F] 20 B1
Rozoy [F] 12 E3
Rue [F] 12 B1
Ruelle–sur–Touvre [F] 24 D3
Ruffec [F] 24 D3
Ruffieux [F] 34 D1
Rugles [F] 10 E4
Rumigny [F] 12 F2
Rumilly [F] 34 D1
Rummen [B] 6 B4
Rumont [F] 20 E1
Rupt [F] 22 C4
Ruurlo [NL] 6 D2

S

Saales [F] 22 D3
Sables–d'Or–les–Pins [F] 8 E3
Sablé–sur–Sarthe [F] 18 A2
Sabres [F] 30 C3
Saeul [L] 14 C3
Sagone [F] 44 A3
Saillagouse [F] 38 C4
Saillans [F] 34 C3
Sains [F] 12 E2
Saint Albain [F] 28 A3
Sainte–Lucie–de–Tallano [F] 44 B4
Sainte–Marie–Siché [F] 44 B3
Saintes [F] 24 C3
Saint Hilaire de la Côte [F] 34 C2
Saissac [F] 38 D2
Salau [F] 38 B3
Salbris [F] 18 E3
Salernes [F] 40 F3
Salers [F] 32 D2
Salice [F] 44 B3
Salies–de–Béarn [F] 30 B4
Salies–du–Salat [F] 38 B2
Salignac–Eyvigues [F] 32 B2
Salins [F] 28 C2
Salins–les–Bains [F] 28 C2
Sallanches [F] 34 E1
Salles [F] 30 C2
Salles [F] 38 C2
Salles–Curan [F] 32 D4
Salon [F] 20 C2
Salon–de–Provence [F] 40 D2

Salses–le–Château [F] 38 E3
Salvagnac [F] 32 B4
Salviac [F] 30 F2
Samadet [F] 30 C4
Samatan [F] 38 B1
Samer [F] 4 B4
Samoëns [F] 34 F1
Sanary–sur–Mer [F] 40 E4
Sancergues [F] 26 D1
Sancerre [F] 18 F4
Sancey–le–Grand [F] 28 D2
Sancoins [F] 26 C2
Sandaucourt [F] 20 F3
Sanguinet [F] 30 B2
Santa Severa [F] 44 C1
Sanxay [F] 24 D2
Sanzay [F] 16 F4
Saorge [F] 42 D2
Saou [F] 34 B4
Sappemeer [NL] 2 E2
Saramon [F] 38 B1
Sari d'Orcino [F] 44 B3
Sarlat–la–Canéda [F] 32 A2
Sarralbe [F] 22 D1
Sarrebourg [F] 22 D2
Sarreguemines [F] 22 D1
Sarre–Union [F] 22 D2
Sarron [F] 30 C4
Sartène [F] 44 B4
Sartilly [F] 10 B3
Sarzeau [F] 16 C2
Sassenage [F] 34 D3
Sassenheim [NL] 2 B4
Saucats [F] 30 C2
Saudron [F] 20 E2
Saugues [F] 32 E2
Saujon [F] 24 B3
Saulieu [F] 26 F1
Sault [F] 40 E1
Saulx [F] 22 B4
Saulxures [F] 22 C4
Saumur [F] 18 A3
Sausheim [F] 22 D4
Sauvagnat [F] 26 B4
Sauve [F] 40 C1
Sauveterre–de–Béarn [F] 36 C2
Sauveterre–de–Guyenne [F] 30 D2
Sauxillanges [F] 32 E1
Sauzé–Vaussais [F] 24 D2
Sauzon [F] 16 B2
Savenay [F] 16 D2
Saverdun [F] 38 C2
Saverne [F] 22 D2
Savignac–les–Eglises [F] 30 F1
Savigny–sur–Braye [F] 18 C2
Savines–le–Lac [F] 34 E4
Scaër [F] 8 C4
Schagen [NL] 2 B3
Scheveningen [NL] 2 A4
Schiermonnikoog [NL] 2 D1
Schilde [B] 6 A3
Schirmeck [F] 22 D3
Schoondijke [NL] 4 E3
Schoonebeek [NL] 2 E3
Schoonhoven [NL] 6 B2
Schoonoord [NL] 2 E3
Scrignac [F] 8 C3
Secondigny [F] 24 C1
Sedan [F] 14 A3
Séderon [F] 40 E1
Sées [F] 10 E4
Segonzac [F] 24 C3
Segré [F] 16 F3
Seiches–sur–le–Loir [F] 18 A2
Seilhac [F] 32 B1

Seilleraye, Château de la– [F] 16 D3
Seissan [F] 36 F2
Sélestat [F] 22 D3
Selles [F] 18 D4
Sellières [F] 28 B2
Selongey [F] 20 E4
Seltz [F] 22 F2
Semur–en–Auxois [F] 20 C4
Sénas [F] 40 D2
Senez [F] 42 B2
Senlis [F] 12 C3
Sennecey–le–Grand [F] 28 A3
Senonches [F] 10 F4
Senones [F] 22 D3
Sens [F] 20 B2
Sens–de–Bretagne [F] 8 F4
Sept–Saulx [F] 12 E4
Serain [F] 12 E2
Seraincourt [F] 12 F3
Seraing [B] 14 B1
Sérent [F] 16 C1
Sermaize–les–Bains [F] 20 E1
Serrant, Château de– [F] 16 F3
Serres [F] 34 C4
Serrières [F] 34 B2
Servian [F] 38 F2
Sète [F] 40 B3
Seurre [F] 28 B2
Sévérac–le–Château [F] 32 D4
Sevrier [F] 34 E1
Seyches [F] 30 E2
Seyne [F] 42 B1
Seyssel [F] 34 D1
Seysses [F] 38 C1
Sézanne [F] 20 C1
's Heerenberg [NL] 6 D2
's–Hertogenbosch [NL] 6 B2
Siddeburen [NL] 2 E2
Siecq [F] 24 C3
Sierck–les–Bains [F] 14 C4
Sierentz [F] 28 F1
Sigean [F] 38 E3
Signes [F] 40 E3
Signy–l'Abbaye [F] 12 F3
Sillé–le–Guillaume [F] 18 B1
Silvacane [F] 40 E2
Simorre [F] 36 F2
Sion [F] 20 F2
Siorac–en–Périgord [F] 30 F2
Sissonne [F] 12 E3
Sisteron [F] 40 F1
Sittard [NL] 6 C4
Sivry–sur–Meuse [F] 14 B4
Six–Fours–les–Plages [F] 40 E4
Sizun [F] 8 B3
Sliedrecht [NL] 6 B2
Sloten [NL] 2 C3
Sluis [NL] 4 E3
Sluis [NL] 4 F2
Smilde [NL] 2 D3
Sneek [NL] 2 C2
Sochaux [F] 28 E1
Soest [NL] 2 C4
Soestdijk [NL] 2 C4
Soignies [B] 12 F1
Soissons [F] 12 D3
Solenzara [F] 44 C3
Solesmes [F] 12 C3
Solesmes, Abbaye de– [F] 18 A2
Solignac [F] 24 F4
Solliès–Pont [F] 40 F4
Solutré, Roche de– [F] 26 F3
Sombernon [F] 28 A1

Sommesous [F] 20 C1
Sommières [F] 40 C2
Sompuis [F] 20 D1
Sore [F] 30 C3
Sorgues [F] 40 D2
Sospel [F] 42 D2
Sotta [F] 44 B4
Souesmes [F] 18 E3
Soufflenheim [F] 22 E2
Souillac [F] 32 B2
Souilly [F] 20 E1
Soulac-sur-Mer [F] 24 B3
Soulaines-Dhuys [F]
20 D2
Soultz [F] 22 D4
Soultz [F] 22 E2
Soumoulou [F] 36 E3
Souppes-sur-Loing [F] 18
F2
Sourdeval [F] 10 C3
Sourdon [F] 12 C2
Sournia [F] 38 D3
Sousceyrac [F] 32 C2
Soustons [F] 30 B3
Souvigny [F] 26 D3
Spa [B] 14 C1
Spakenburg [NL] 2 C4
Spijkenisse [NL] 4 F2
Spincourt [F] 14 B4
Stadskanaal [NL] 2 E3
St-Affrique [F] 38 E1
St-Agnant [F] 24 B3
St-Agrève [F] 34 B3
St-Aignan [F] 16 E2
St-Aignan [F] 18 D4
Stainville [F] 20 E2
St-Alban [F] 32 E3
St-Amand-en-Puisaye [F]
20 A4
St-Amand-les-Eaux [F] 12
E1
St-Amand-Longpré [F] 18
C3
St-Amand-Montrond [F] 26
C2
St-Amans [F] 32 E3
St-Amant-Roche-Savine [F]
32 F1
St-Ambroix [F] 32 F4
St-Amé [F] 22 C3
St-Amour [F] 28 B3
St-André [F] 12 A4
St-André-de-Cubzac [F] 30
D1
St-André-les-Alpes [F] 42
B2
St Annaparochie [NL] 2 D2
St-Anthème [F] 32 F1
St-Antoine [F] 34 C2
St.-Antoine, Chapelle– [F] 36
C2
St-Antonin-Noble-Val [F] 32
B4
St.-Antonino [F] 44 B2
St-Août [F] 26 B2
St-Astier [F] 30 E1
St-Aubane [F] 42 C2
St-Auban-sur-l'Ouvèze [F]
40 E1
St-Aubin-d'Aubigné [F]
8 F4
St-Aubin-du-Cormier [F] 8
F4
St-Aubin-sur-Mer [F]
10 D2
St.-Augustin, Château de–
[F] 26 C2
St-Aulaye [F] 30 E1
Stavelot [B] 14 C2
Stavenisse [NL] 4 F2
Staveren [NL] 2 C3

St-Avold [F] 22 D1
St-Aygulf [F] 42 B3
St-Bard [F] 26 B4
St-Béat [F] 36 F4
St-Beauzély [F] 32 D4
St-Benin [F] 26 D2
St-Benoît [F] 24 F2
St-Benoît-sur-Loire [F] 18
E3
St-Bertrand-de-Comminges
[F] 36 F3
St.-Blaise [F] 40 D3
St-Blin [F] 20 E3
St-Bonnet [F] 34 D4
St-Bonnet-de-Joux [F] 26
F3
St-Bonnet-en-Champsaur
[F] 34 D4
St-Bonnet-le-Château [F] 32
F2
St-Brevin-les-Pins [F] 16
C3
St-Brice-en-Coglès [F] 10
B4
St-Brieuc [F] 8 D3
St-Calais [F] 18 C2
St-Cast-le-Guildo [F] 8 E3
St-Céré [F] 32 B2
St-Cernin [F] 32 C2
St-Chamas [F] 40 D3
St-Chamond [F] 34 B2
St-Chély-d'Apcher [F] 32 E3
St-Chély-d'Aubrac [F] 32 D3
St-Chinian [F] 38 E2
St.Christophe-en-Oisans [F]
34 D3
St-Ciers [F] 24 B4
St-Cirq-Lapopie [F] 32 B3
St.-Clair [F] 10 D2
St-Clar [F] 30 E4
St-Claud [F] 24 C3
St-Claude [F] 28 C3
St-Clément-sur-Durance [F]
34 E4
St-Côme-d'Olt [F] 32 D3
St-Cyprien [F] 30 F2
St-Cyprien-Plage [F] 38 E4
St-Denis [F] 12 C4
St-Denis-d'Oléron [F] 24 B2
St-Denis d'Orques [F] 18 A2
St-Didier-en-Velay [F] 34
A2
St-Dié [F] 22 D3
St-Dizier [F] 20 E2
St-Donat-sur-l'Herbasse [F]
34 B3
Ste-Anne-d'Auray [F] 16 B1
Ste-Anne-la-Palud [F] 8 B3
Ste.-Barbe [F] 22 D2
Ste-Croix-Volvestre [F] 38
B2
Steenbergen [NL] 4 F3
Ste.-Engrâce [F] 36 E4
Ste-Enimie [F] 32 E4
Steenvoorde [F] 4 C4
Steenwijk [NL] 2 D3
Ste-Foy-la-Grande [F] 30 E2
Ste-Gauburge-Ste-Colombe
[F] 10 E4
Ste-Egrève [F] 34 D2
Ste-Hélène [F] 30 C1
Ste-Hermine [F] 24 B1
Ste.-Jalle [F] 40 E1
Ste-Livrade-sur-Lot [F] 30
E3
Stellendam [NL] 4 F2
Ste-Eloy-les-Mines [F] 26 C3
Ste-Marie-aux-Mines [F] 22
D3
Ste.-Marie-de-Campan [F]
36 E3

Ste-Maure-de-Touraine [F]
18 B4
Ste-Maxime [F] 42 B3
Ste-Menehould [F] 14 A4
Ste-Mère-du-Mont [F] 10
C2
Ste-Mère-Eglise [F] 10 C2
St-Emilion [F] 30 D2
Stenay [F] 14 B3
Ste-Sévère [F] 26 B2
Stes-Maries-de-la-Mer [F]
40 C3
St. Estèphe [F] 24 B4
Ste-Suzanne [F] 18 A1
St-Étienne [F] 40 F2
St-Étienne [F] 34 B2
St-Étienne-de-Baïgorry [F]
36 C2
St-Étienne-de-St-Geoirs [F]
34 C2
St-Étienne-de-Tinée [F] 42
C2
St-Etienne-les-Orgues [F]
40 F2
Ste-Tulle [F] 40 E2
St-Fargeau [F] 20 A3
St.-Fiacre [F] 8 C4
St-Firmin [F] 34 D3
St-Florent [F] 44 C1
St-Florent [F] 16 E3
St-Florent [F] 26 B1
St.-Florent-des-Bois [F] 16
D4
St-Florentin [F] 20 B3
St-Flour [F] 32 E2
St-Fort-sur-Gironde [F] 24
B4
St-Fulgent [F] 16 E4
St-Galmier [F] 34 B1
St-Gaudens [F] 36 F3
St-Gaultier [F] 26 A2
St-Geniez-d'Olt [F] 32 D3
St-Genis-de-Saintonge [F]
24 C4
St-Genix-sur-Guiers [F] 34
D2
St-Georges [F] 16 F3
St-Georges-de-Didonne [F]
24 B3
St. Georges-on-Couzan [F]
32 F1
St-Geours-de-Maremne [F]
30 B4
St-Germain [F] 24 F4
St-Germain [F] 12 B4
St-Germain-de-Joux [F] 28
B4
St-Germain-des-Fossés [F]
26 D3
St-Germain-des-Vaux [F] 10
B1
St-Germain-du-Bois [F] 28
B3
St-Germain-du-Plain [F] 28
A3
St-Germain-Laval [F] 26 E4
St-Germain-Lembron [F] 32
E1
St-Germain-l'Herm [F] 32
E1
St-Germain-Plage [F] 10 B2
St-Germer-de-Fly [F] 12 B3
St-Gervais [F] 38 E2
St-Gervais-d'Auvergne [F]
26 C3
St-Gervais-les-Bains [F] 34
E1
St-Géry [F] 32 B3
St-Gildas-des-Bois [F] 16
D2
St-Gilles [F] 40 C2

St-Gilles-Croix-de-Vie [F]
16 C4
St-Girons [F] 38 B2
St-Girons-en-Marensin [F]
30 B3
St-Girons-Plage [F] 30 B3
St-Gobain [F] 12 D3
St-Gorgon-Main [F] 28 D2
St-Guénolé [F] 8 A4
St-Guilhem-le-Desert [F] 40
B2
St. Hilaire Cottes [F] 4 C4
St-Hilaire-de-Villefranche
[F] 24 C3
St-Hilaire-du-Harcouët [F]
10 C3
St-Hippolyte [F] 28 D2
St-Hippolyte-du-Fort [F] 40
B1
St-Honoré [F] 26 E2
St-Hubert [B] 14 B2
Stiens [NL] 2 D2
St-Jacut [F] 8 E3
St-James [F] 10 B3
St-Jean-Brévelay [F] 16 C1
St-Jean-Cap-Ferrat [F] 42
C3
St-Jean-d'Angély [F] 24 C3
St-Jean-de-Bournay [F] 34
C2
St-Jean-de-Losne [F] 28 B2
St-Jean-de-Luz [F] 36 B2
St-Jean-de-Maurienne [F]
34 E3
St-Jean-de-Monts [F] 16 C3
St-Jean-du-Bruel [F] 38 F1
St-Jean-du-Gard [F] 40 C1
St-Jean-du-Liget, Chapelle–
[F] 18 C4
St-Jean-en-Royans [F] 34
C3
St-Jean-le-Thomas [F] 10
B3
St-Jean-Pied-de-Port [F] 36
C2
St. Jeans-d' Arves [F] 34 E3
St-Jeoire [F] 28 D4
St-Jorioz [F] 34 E1
St-Jory [F] 38 C1
St-Jouan-de-l'Isle [F] 8 E4
St-Jouin-de-Marnes [F] 18
A4
St-Juéry [F] 38 D1
St-Julien [F] 38 B2
St-Julien [F] 28 B3
St-Julien-Chapteuil [F] 32
F2
St-Julien-de-Vouvantes [F]
16 E2
St-Julien-en-Beauchêne [F]
34 C4
St-Julien-en-Genevois [F]
28 C4
St-Julien-l'Ars [F] 24 E2
St-Junien [F] 24 E3
St-Just-en-Chaussée [F] 12
C3
St-Just-en-Chevalet [F] 26
D4
St-Justin [F] 30 C3
St-Lary-Soulan [F] 36 E4
St-Laurent [F] 24 E3
St-Laurent [F] 10 C2
St-Laurent-en-Grandvaux
[F] 28 C3
St-Laurent-les-Bains [F] 32
F3
St-Laurent-Médoc [F] 24 B4
St-Leger [F] 26 E2
St.-Léon, Chapelle– [F]
22 D2

St-Léonard-de-Noblat [F] 24
F3
St-Leu-d'Esserent [F] 12 C3
St-Lizier [F] 38 B2
St-Lô [F] 10 C2
St-Louis [F] 28 F1
St-Loup-sur-Semouse [F]
22 C4
St-Lunaire [F] 8 E3
St-Lys [F] 38 B1
St-Macaire [F] 30 D2
St-Maclou [F] 10 E2
St-Maixent-l'Ecole [F] 24 D2
St-Malo [F] 8 E3
St-Mamest [F] 30 E2
St. Marcel [F] 34 E2
St-Marcellin [F] 34 C3
St-Marcellin-en-Forez [F]
34 A2
St-Mars-la-Jaille [F] 16 E2
St. Martin [F] 16 C1
St-Martin-d'Auxigny [F] 18
E4
St-Martin-de-Londres [F] 40
B2
St. Martin-d' Entraunes [F]
42 C2
St-Martin-de-Ré [F] 24 B2
St.-Martin-du-Canigou [F]
38 D4
St-Martin-Vésubie [F] 42 C2
St-Martory [F] 38 B2
St-Mathieu [F] 24 E4
St.-Mathieu, Pointe de– [F] 8
A3
St-Mathieu-de-Tréviers [F]
40 B2
St.Maurice la Sotterraine [F]
24 F3
St-Maurice-Navacelles [F]
40 B2
St Maurice-sur-Moselle [F]
22 C4
St-Maximin-la-Ste-Baume
[F] 40 F3
St.-Méen [F] 8 E4
St.-Michel-de Cuxa [F] 38
D4
St-Michel-de-Maurienne [F]
34 E3
St.Michel de Rieufret [F] 30
C2
St-Michel-en-Grève [F] 8
C2
St-Michel-en-l'Herm [F] 24
B2
St-Michel-Mont-Mercure [F]
16 E4
St-Mihiel [F] 20 F1
St-Morand [F] 28 E1
St-Nazaire [F] 16 C2
St-Nectaire [F] 32 E1
St.-Nicodème [F] 8 D4
St-Nicolas [F] 16 D2
St Nicolas-de-Port [F] 22
C2
St-Nicolas-du-Pélem [F] 8
D3
St-Niklaas [B] 4 F3
St Oedenrode [NL] 6 C3
St-Omer [F] 4 C4
St.-Oswald [F] 14 C4
St-Ouen [F] 12 C1
St-Palais [F] 36 C2
St-Palais-sur-Mer [F] 24 B3
St-Pardoux-la-Rivière [F] 24
E4
St-Paul [F] 42 C3
St-Paul [F] 42 C1
St-Paul-Cap-de-Joux [F]
38 D1

St-Paul-de-Fenouillet [F] 38 D3
St-Pauliene [F] 32 F2
St-Paul-lès-Dax [F] 30 B4
St-Pé [F] 36 D3
St-Péray [F] 34 B3
St-Père [F] 20 B4
St-Père-en-Retz [F] 16 C3
St-Philbert [F] 16 D3
St-Pierre-d'Albigny [F] 34 E2
St-Pierre-de-Chartreuse [F] 34 D2
St-Pierre-de-Chignac [F] 30 F1
St.-Pierre d'Extravache [F] 34 E3
St-Pierre-d'Oléron [F] 24 B2
St-Pierre-Église [F] 10 C1
St-Pierre-le-Moûtier [F] 26 D2
St-Pierre-Quiberon [F] 16 B2
St-Pierre-sur-Dives [F] 10 D3
St-Pois [F] 10 C3
St-Pol-de-Léon [F] 8 C2
St-Pons [F] 38 E2
St-Pons-de-Thomieres [F] 38 E2
St-Porchaire [F] 24 B3
St-Pourçain [F] 26 D3
St.Priest [F] 34 C1
St-Privat [F] 32 C2
St-Quay-Portrieux [F] 8 D3
St-Quentin [F] 12 D2
St-Rambert [F] 34 A2
St-Rambert-d'Albon [F] 34 B2
St-Rambert-en-Bugey [F] 34 C1
St-Raphaël [F] 42 B3
Strasbourg [F] 22 E2
St-Rémy-de-Provence [F] 40 D2
St-Renan [F] 8 B3
St-Riquier [F] 12 C1
St.-Roman, Abbaye de- [F] 40 D2
St-Rome-de-Tarn [F] 38 E1
St.-Sabin, Chapelle- [F] 30 D3
St-Saëns [F] 12 A2
St-Satur [F] 18 F4
St-Saturnin-lès-Apt [F] 40 E2
St-Saulge [F] 26 D1
St-Sauvant [F] 24 D2
St-Sauveur-en-Puisaye [F] 20 B3
St-Sauveur-le-Vicomte [F] 10 B2
St-Sauveur-sur-Tinée [F] 42 C2
St-Savin [F] 30 D1
St-Savin [F] 24 E2
St-Seine-l'Abbaye [F] 20 D4
St-Sernin-sur-Rance [F] 38 E1
St-Sever [F] 30 C4
St-Sever [F] 10 C3
St-Sulpice [F] 38 C1
St. Sulpice-Les-Feuilles [F] 24 F2
St-Symphorien [F] 30 C2
St-Symphorien-de-Lay [F] 26 E4
St-Symphorien-d'Ozon [F] 34 C1
St-Symphorien-sur-Coise [F] 34 B1
St-Thégonnec [F] 8 C3

St-Thiébault [F] 20 E3
St-Trivier-de-Courtes [F] 28 B3
St-Tropez [F] 42 B3
St.-Ulrich, Château- [F] 22 D3
St-Vaast-la-Hougue [F] 10 C1
St-Valery-en-Caux [F] 10 F1
St-Valery-sur-Somme [F] 12 B1
St-Vallier-de-Thiey [F] 42 C3
St-Vallier-sur-Rhône [F] 34 B2
St-Vaury [F] 26 A3
St-Véran [F] 34 E4
St-Vincent, Grotte de- [F] 40 F1
St-Vincent-de-Tyrosse [F] 30 B4
St. Vincent-du-Lorouër [F] 18 C2
St-Vincent-les-Forts [F] 42 B1
St Vith [B] 14 C2
St-Vivien-de-Médoc [F] 24 B4
St-Wandrille [F] 10 F2
St-Yan [F] 26 E3
St-Yorre [F] 26 D4
St-Yrieix-la-Perche [F] 24 E4
Sugères [F] 32 E1
Suippes [F] 12 F4
Sully [F] 26 F2
Sully-sur-Loire [F] 18 E3
Surgères [F] 24 C2
Surtainville [F] 10 B1
Survilliers [F] 12 C3
Suscinio, Château de- [F] 16 C2
Sutrieu [F] 34 D1
Swalmen [NL] 6 C4

T

Tagenac [F] 32 D2
Taillebois [F] 10 D3
Tain-l'Hermitage [F] 34 B3
Taizé [F] 26 F3
Talcy [F] 18 D3
Tallard [F] 34 D4
Talloires [F] 34 E1
Talmont [F] 24 B3
Talmont-St-Hilaire [F] 24 A1
Tancarville [F] 10 E2
Taninges [F] 28 D4
Tanlay [F] 20 C3
Taponas [F] 26 F4
Tarare [F] 26 E4
Tarascon [F] 40 D2
Tarascon-sur-Ariège [F] 38 C3
Tarbes [F] 36 E3
Tardets-Sorholus [F] 36 C3
Tarnos [F] 30 A4
Tartas [F] 30 B3
Tauves [F] 32 D1
Tavaux [F] 28 B2
Tavernes [F] 40 F3
Tegelen [NL] 6 C3
Teillay [F] 16 E2
Teillet [F] 38 D1
Temse [B] 4 F3
Tence [F] 34 A2

Tende [F] 42 D2
Ter Apel [NL] 2 E3
Tergnier [F] 12 D3
Termes-d'Armagnac [F] 30 D4
Terneuzen [NL] 4 E3
Terrasson-la-Villedieu [F] 32 B2
Tervuren [B] 4 F4
Tessy sur-Vire [F] 10 C3
Thaumiers [F] 26 C2
Thénezay [F] 24 D1
Thenon [F] 30 F1
Théoule [F] 42 C3
Thérouanne [F] 4 C4
Theuley [F] 20 E4
Theux [B] 14 C1
Thevet-St-Julien [F] 26 B2
Theze [F] 36 D2
Thiaucourt-Regniéville [F] 20 F1
Thiberville [F] 10 E3
Thiélbemont-Farémont [F] 20 D2
Thiers [F] 26 D4
Thionville [F] 14 C4
Thirette [F] 28 B4
Thivars [F] 18 D1
Thiviers [F] 24 E4
Thizy [F] 26 E4
Thoissey [F] 26 F4
Thônes [F] 34 E1
Thonon [F] 28 D4
Thonon-les-Bains [F] 28 D4
Thorens-Glières, Château de- [F] 34 E1
Thoronet, Abbaye du- [F] 40 F3
Thors [F] 20 D2
Thouarcé [F] 16 F3
Thouars [F] 16 F4
Thueyts [F] 32 F3
Thuin [B] 12 F1
Thuir [F] 38 E4
Thuret [F] 26 D4
Thury-Harcourt [F] 10 D3
Tibarrié [F] 38 E1
Tiel [NL] 6 C2
Tielt [B] 4 D4
Tiercé [F] 16 F2
Tignes [F] 34 F2
Tilburg [NL] 6 B3
Til-Châtel [F] 20 E4
Tinchebray [F] 10 C3
Tiuccia [F] 44 A3
Tizzano [F] 44 B4
Tombebœuf [F] 30 E3
Tonnay-Boutonne [F] 24 C2
Tonnay-Charente [F] 24 B2
Tonneins [F] 30 E3
Tonnerre [F] 20 C3
Tonquédec, Château de- [F] 8 C2
Torhout [B] 4 D3
Torigni-sur-Vire [F] 10 C3
Tôtes [F] 12 A2
Toucy [F] 20 B3
Touffou [F] 24 E2
Toul [F] 20 F2
Toulon [F] 40 F4
Toulon sur Allier [F] 26 D3
Toulon-sur-Arroux [F] 26 E2
Toulouse [F] 38 C1
Tourcoing [F] 4 D4
Tourmalet, Col du- [F] 36 E3
Tournan [F] 20 A1
Tournay [F] 36 E3
Tournon [F] 34 B3
Tournon-d'Agenais [F] 30 F3
Tournon-St-Martin [F] 24 F1

Tournus [F] 28 A3
Tours [F] 18 C3
Tourves [F] 40 F3
Toury [F] 18 E2
Toutes Aures, Col en- [F] 42 B2
Trabuc, Grottes de- [F] 40 C1
Trappe d'Aiguebelle, Monastère de la- [F] 34 B4
Trappes [F] 12 B4
Travo [F] 44 C3
Tréban [F] 26 D3
Trébeurden [F] 8 C2
Tréboul [F] 8 B3
Trecesson, Château de- [F] 16 D1
Trégastel [F] 8 C2
Tréguier [F] 8 D2
Treignac [F] 26 A4
Trept [F] 34 C1
Trets [F] 40 E3
Tréveray [F] 20 E2
Trévoux [F] 26 F4
Trezelles [F] 26 D3
Triaize [F] 24 B1
Triaucourt-en-Argonne [F] 20 E1
Trie [F] 36 E3
Trignac [F] 16 C2
Trinité, Ermitage de la- [F] 44 B4
Troarn [F] 10 D3
Trois Fontaines, Abbaye des- [F] 20 E2
Trois-Ponts [B] 14 C2
Trôo [F] 18 C2
Trouville [F] 10 E2
Troyes [F] 20 C2
Truchtersheim [F] 22 E2
Trun [F] 10 D3
Tuchan [F] 38 E3
Tuffé [F] 18 C2
Tulle [F] 32 B1
Tullins [F] 34 C2
Tumulus de Gavrinis [F] 16 B2
Tuornoel, Château de- [F] 26 C4
Turckheim [F] 22 D3
Turenne [F] 32 B2
Turnhout [B] 6 B3
Tzummarum [NL] 2 C2

U

Uckange [F] 14 C4
Uddel [NL] 2 C4
Uden [NL] 6 C3
Ugine [F] 34 E2
Uithoorn [NL] 2 B4
Uithuizen [NL] 2 E2
Urbise [F] 26 E3
Urçay [F] 26 C2
Urdos [F] 36 D3
Uriage-les-Bains [F] 34 D3
Urk [NL] 2 C3
Ury [F] 18 F2
Ussé [F] 18 B3
Ussel [F] 32 C1
Usson-du-Poitou [F] 24 E2
Usson-les-Bains [F] 38 D3
Ustaritz [F] 30 A4
Utrecht [NL] 2 B4
Uzel [F] 8 D3
Uzerche [F] 32 B1

Uzès [F] 40 C1
Uzeste [F] 30 D2

V

Vaas [F] 18 B2
Vaassen [NL] 2 D4
Vaiges [F] 18 A1
Vailly [F] 18 F4
Vailly [F] 12 D3
Vaison-la-Romaine [F] 40 D1
Valberg [F] 42 C2
Valbonnais [F] 34 D3
Valensole [F] 40 F2
Val-Claret [F] 34 F2
Valdahon [F] 28 D2
Val d'Esquières [F] 42 B3
Val d'Isère [F] 34 F2
Val-d'Izé [F] 10 B4
Valençay [F] 18 D4
Valence [F] 30 D4
Valence [F] 30 E4
Valence [F] 34 B3
Valence d'Albigeois [F] 32 C4
Valenciennes [F] 12 E1
Valentigney [F] 28 E1
Valkenswaard [NL] 6 C3
Vallenhove [NL] 2 D3
Valleraugue [F] 40 B1
Vallet [F] 16 E3
Valloire [F] 34 E3
Vallon-en-Sully [F] 26 C2
Vallon-Pont-d'Arc [F] 34 A4
Vallorcine [F] 34 F1
Vallouise [F] 34 E3
Valmigère [F] 38 D3
Valmorel [F] 34 E2
Valognes [F] 10 C1
Valras-Plage [F] 38 F3
Valréas [F] 34 B4
Vals-les-Bains [F] 34 A3
Val-Suzon [F] 28 B1
Val Thorens [F] 34 E3
Vandenesse [F] 26 E2
Vannes [F] 16 C1
Varades [F] 16 E3
Varages [F] 40 F3
Varces [F] 34 D3
Varengeville-sur-Mer [F] 12 A1
Varennes-en-Argonne [F] 14 A4
Varennes-sur-Allier [F] 26 D3
Varilhes [F] 38 C3
Vars [F] 34 E4
Varsseveld [NL] 6 D2
Varzy [F] 20 B4
Vasles [F] 24 D1
Vassy [F] 10 C3
Vatan [F] 18 D4
Vaucelles, Abbaye de- [F] 12 D2
Vauclaix [F] 26 E1
Vaucouleurs [F] 20 F2
Vaudoy en Brie [F] 20 B1
Vauvenargues [F] 40 E3
Vauvert [F] 40 C2
Vauville [F] 10 B1
Vauvillers [F] 20 F3
Vaux-Le Vicomte [F] 18 F1
Vayrac [F] 32 B2
Veendam [NL] 2 E2
Veenendaal [NL] 6 C2
Veere [NL] 4 E2

Veghel [NL] 6 C3
Veldhoven [NL] 6 B3
Velp [NL] 6 C2
Venaco [F] 44 B2
Vence [F] 42 C3
Vendargues [F] 40 B2
Vendays-Montalivet [F] 24 B4
Vendeuvre [F] 20 D2
Vendôme [F] 18 C2
Vendranges [F] 26 E4
Venlo [NL] 6 D3
Venoy [F] 20 B3
Venray [NL] 6 C3
Ventadour, Château de- [F]
    32 C1
Ventiseri [F] 44 B3
Verberie [F] 12 C3
Verdelles, Château de- [F] 18
    A2
Verdun [F] 14 B4
Verfeil [F] 38 C1
Verghia [F] 44 A3
Vergt [F] 30 E2
Vermenton [F] 20 B3
Vernet [F] 38 C2
Vernet-les-Bains [F] 38 D4
Verneuil-sur-Avre [F] 10 F4
Vernon [F] 12 A3
Verny [F] 22 C1
Verrières-de-Joux [F] 28 D3
Versailles [F] 12 B4
Versols-et-Lapeyre [F] 38 E1
Verteillac [F] 24 D4
Vertou [F] 16 D3
Vertus [F] 20 C1
Verviers [B] 14 C1
Vervins [F] 12 E2
Verzy [F] 12 E4
Vescovato [F] 44 C2
Vesoul [F] 20 F4
Veules-les-Roses [F] 10 F1
Veulettes-sur-Mer [F] 10 F1
Veurne (Furnes) [B] 4 C3
Veynes [F] 34 D4
Veyrier [F] 34 E1
Vézelay [F] 20 B4
Vézelise [F] 22 C2
Vézénobres [F] 40 C1
Viais [F] 16 D3
Vianden [L] 14 C3
Viane [F] 38 E1
Vianen [NL] 6 B2
Vianne [F] 30 D3
Vias [F] 38 F2
Vibraye [F] 18 C2
Vic [F] 32 E1
Vicdessos [F] 38 C3
Vic-en-Bigorre [F] 36 E2
Vic-Fezensac [F] 30 D4
Vichy [F] 26 D3
Vico [F] 44 B2
Vic-sur-Aisne [F] 12 D3

Vic-sur-Cère [F] 32 D2
Victoire, Abbaye de la- [F] 12
    C3
Vidauban [F] 42 B3
Vieland [NL] 2 C2
Vielsalm [B] 14 C2
Vienne [F] 34 B2
Vierville [F] 10 C2
Vierzon [F] 18 E4
Vieux-Boucau-les-Bains [F]
    30 A3
Vif [F] 34 D3
Vigneulles [F] 20 F1
Vignory [F] 20 E2
Vihiers [F] 16 F3
Village, Roche aux- [F] 14
    A2
Villagrains [F] 30 C2
Villaines-la-Juhel [F] 10 D4
Villandraut [F] 30 C2
Villandry [F] 18 B3
Villard-de-Lans [F] 34 C3
Villardebelle [F] 38 D3
Villars [F] 42 C2
Villars-les-Dombes [F] 28
    A4
Villars-sur-Var [F] 42 C2
Villé [F] 22 D3
Villebois-Lavalette [F] 24 D4
Villedieu-les-Poêles [F] 10
    C3
Ville-en-Tardenois [F] 12 E4
Villefagnan [F] 24 D3
Villefontaine [F] 34 C2
Villefort [F] 32 F4
Villefranche [F] 42 C2
Villefranche-d'Albigeois [F]
    38 D1
Villefranche-de-Conflent [F]
    38 D4
Villefranche-de-Lauragais
    [F] 38 C2
Villefranche-de-Lonchat [F]
    30 D2
Villefranche-de-Panat [F] 32
    C4
Villefranche-de-Rouergue [F]
    32 B3
Villefranche-du-Périgord [F]
    30 F3
Villefranche-sur-Cher [F] 18
    D4
Villefranche-sur-Saône [F]
    26 F4
Villegats [F] 24 D3
Villemur [F] 32 A4
Villenauxe-la-Grande [F] 20
    C1
Villeneuve [F] 32 C3
Villeneuve [F] 40 D2
Villeneuve-de-Berg [F]
    34 B4

Villeneuve-de-Marsan [F] 30
    C4
Villeneuve-l'Archevêque [F]
    20 B2
Villeneuve-Loubet [F] 42 C3
Villeneuve-sur-Allier [F] 26
    D2
Villeneuve-sur-Lot [F] 30 E3
Villeneuve-sur-Yonne [F] 20
    B2
Villeréal [F] 30 E2
Villers [B] 14 A1
Villers [F] 10 E2
Villers-Bocage [F] 10 D3
Villers-Bretonneux [F] 12 C2
Villers-Cotterêts [F] 12 D3
Villersexel [F] 28 D1
Villers-le-Lac [F] 28 D2
Villers-St-Georges [F] 20 B1
Villerville [F] 10 E2
Ville-sur-Illon [F] 22 C3
Villon [F] 20 C3
Vimoutiers [F] 10 E3
Vinay [F] 34 C2
Vinça [F] 38 D4
Vingrau [F] 38 E3
Vinon-sur-Verdon [F] 40 F2
Violès [F] 40 D1
Vire [F] 10 C3
Viré [F] 28 A3
Vire Court [F] 8 B4
Viriat [F] 28 B4
Virieu [F] 34 C2
Virieu-le-Grand [F] 34 D1
Virton [B] 14 B3
Visé [B] 14 C1
Vitré [F] 16 E1
Vitry-le-François [F] 20 D1
Vitteaux [F] 20 C4
Vittel [F] 20 F3
Vivario [F] 44 B2
Vivier, Château du- [F] 20 A1
Viviers [F] 34 B4
Vivonne [F] 24 D2
Vizille [F] 34 D3
Vizzavona [F] 44 B3
Vlaardingen [NL] 4 F2
Vlagtwedd [NL] 2 E3
Vlissingen [NL] 4 E3
Void [F] 20 F2
Voiron [F] 34 D2
Voise [F] 18 E1
Voix [F] 40 F2
Volendam [NL] 2 B3
Volkel [NL] ... (Volvic) [F] 26 C4
Voorschoten [NL] 2 A4
Voorst [NL] 2 D4
Voreppe [F] 34 D2
Vorey [F] 32 F2
Vouillé [F] 24 D1
Vouvant [F] 24 C1
Vouvray [F] 18 C3

Voves [F] 18 D2
Vresse [B] 14 A2
Vriezenveen [NL] 2 E4
Vrigny [F] 12 E4
Vroomshoop [NL] 2 D4
Vroville [F] 22 C3
Vue [F] 16 D3
Vught [NL] 6 B3

Waalwijk [NL] 6 B2
Wageningen [NL] 6 C2
Walcourt [B] 12 F2
Wangenbourg [F] 22 D2
Waregem [B] 4 D4
Waremme [F] 14 B1
Warnsveld [NL] 6 D2
Wasigenstein, Château de-
    [F] 22 E1
Wasselonne [F] 22 E2
Wassenaar [NL] 2 A4
Wasserbillig [L] 14 C3
Wassy [F] 20 E2
Watten [F] 4 C4
Waulsort [B] 14 A2
Weert [NL] 6 C3
Well [NL] 6 C3
Wellin [B] 14 B2
Wemperhaardt [L] 14 C2
Wépion [B] 14 A1
Werbomont [B] 14 C2
Westende-Bad [B] 4 D3
Westerlo [B] 6 B4
Westkapelle [NL] 4 E2
West-Terschelling [NL] 2 C1
Wetteren [B] 4 E4
Wierden [NL] 2 D4
Wijhe [NL] 2 D4
Willebroek [B] 4 F4
Willemstad [NL] 4 F2
Wilsin [NL] 2 B4
Wiltz [L] 14 C2
Wimereux [F] 4 B4
Winschoten [NL] 2 E2
Winsum [NL] 2 E2
Winterswijk [NL] 6 E2
Wissant [F] 4 B3
Wissembourg [F] 22 E1
Woerden [NL] 2 B4
Woerth [F] 22 E2
Woesten [B] 4 D4
Wolvega [NL] 2 D3
Workum [NL] 2 C2
Wormerveer [NL] 2 B3
Wormhout [F] 4 C4
Wuustwezel [B] 6 A3

Xertigny [F] 22 C3
Xhoffraix [B] 14 C1

Ychoux [F] 30 B2
Yenne [F] 34 D2
Yerville [F] 10 F2
Yport [F] 10 E2
Ypres (Ieper) [B] 4 D4
Yquem, Château- [F] 30
    D2
Yrouerre [F] 20 C3
Yssandon, Puy d'- [F] 32
    B1
Yssingeaux [F] 32 F2
Yvetot [F] 10 F2
Yvoir [B] 14 A1
Yvoire [F] 28 C4

Zaandam [NL] 2 B3
Zaltbommel [NL] 6 B2
Zandvoort [NL] 2 B3
Zeebrugge [B] 4 D3
Zeist [NL] 2 C4
Zelhem [NL] 6 D2
Zelzate [B] 4 E3
Zevenaar [NL] 6 D2
Zevenbergen [NL] 6
    A2
Zicavo [F] 44 B3
Zierikzee [NL] 4 E2
Zijpe [NL] 4 F2
Zoetermeer [NL] 2 A4
Zolder [B] 6 B4
Zonza [F] 44 B3
Zoutkamp [NL] 2 D2
Zoutleeuw [B] 6 B4
Zuani [F] 44 C2
Zuidhorn [NL] 2 D2
Zuidlaren [NL] 2 E2
Zundert [NL] 6 A3
Zutphen [NL] 6 D2
Zwijndrecht [NL] 6 B2
Zwolle [NL] 2 D3

X

W

Y

Z